VARIATIONS ON PAINTING A ROOM

Designed & Published by SKYSILL Press
3 Gervase Gardens Clifton Village Nottingham NG11 8LZ
in the Year of the Rabbit 2011

VARIATIONS ON PAINTING A ROOM:
POEMS 2000-2010

ALAN BAKER

skysillpress.blogspot.com

ISBN 978-1-907489-05-1

ACKNOWLEDGEMENTS

Some of the poems in this collection have previously appeared in the following magazines: *The Affectionate Punch, Assent, Envoi, Eyewear, Gists & Piths, Great Works, Hamilton Stone Review, The Interpreter's House, Iota, Logololia, nth Position, Poetry Nottingham, Shadowtrain, Shearsman, Staple, Stride, Tears in the Fence*. Thanks to the editors.

Other parts of this book have been published in pamphlet form by the following publishers, to whom grateful acknowledgement is made:

Not Bondi Beach (Leafe Press, 2002)
The Strange City (Secretariat Books, 2006). Jayne Mansfield
Hotel February (Bamboo Books, 2008). Bob Rissman
The World Seen from the Air (Skysill Press, 2009)

For their writerly support, I'd like to thank my good friends Clive Allen, John Bloomberg-Rissman, Adrian Buckner and John Lucas.

Special thanks to Sam Ward, for making this book happen.

CONTENTS

IV. Hotel February / 69

V. The Book of Random Access / 87

VI. Everyday Songs / 153

Notes / 185

Grey sky, grey sea. And there they were. They might have been seals I thought, showing off their survival skills in the freezing waters, until one of them rose like a sea-nymph, riding the surf, as if it were Bondi, not Roker beach, and conch-shells lay in the sand, not snow.

As the surfers wobbled, on hunkers first, then arms out, like ballerinas, the walkers who had huddled to watch them by the pier's frosted railings broke into applause, and forgave them: forgave them for not being seals, not welding ships, not trawling fish and not mining coal; forgave them because the shoreline of abandoned boarding houses and no shipyards wasn't their fault; forgave them because there they were riding along on the crest of a wave, at Monkwearmouth Harbour, Sunderland, Tyne and Wear, SR6, United Kingdom (E.C. Region 1056).

A DARKENED COUNTRY

How is it then, that thou art so quickly
turned aside, for thou
art now out of the way.

Living rooms flicker
to *The World About Us*
& in the suburbs all about us

creep intimations
of immortal soap-stars
lonesome hobos

delirious lottery winners
economic false dawns
& early nights

a darkened country
where money doesn't grow on trees
& doing your best

with your foot forward
on that shifting path
might take you by surprise

standing your eyes smarting
your rucksack
prodding your back

as if you'd set out
on a journey to the cold mirror
of the open sky

without a study of light
& its behaviour, how it gleams
in unpromised places

when the street lights beckon
across a valley
& the stocks begin to rise

in the gardens that you pass
in the dusk
on that first difficult journey

ONE WHO TRAVELLED TO FIND WHAT LISTENING MEANT

for Rachel

Wrapped chrysalis curled
against pane-sparkling
rain and night

tiny pupil whose schooling
dialtes to take
the wanderer's every turn

by Tom Thumb views
the wolf's stomach
enthralled   while I

in thrall
to a passing season
under your hill

hardly recognising
who I am seeing will be
soon grown

at the speed-of-light
watching see language
grow & wonder

who you are & where
you came from & how
can I attain or ever

return to follow
a fox's russet
through a gap in the hedge

learn industry
of the ant
or profligacy

in the spreading waters
miraculous memory
flooding ridge-and-furrow

let you tell me a story
of 'the wind whistling through
the forest one bright summer's day'

Begin

CHILWELL

Here at the hill's foot
'the well where children gather'
gather for harvest

gather for games
or outside cottages where mothers
tend their nurslings

heaved to health or lost time & again
where the Trent
spreads over meadows

time & again night drags deeper
its heat   the tug of fever
untreatable but by time & chance

loosens their hold   falling
falling   holding hands
all in a row   all fall down

into mud where meanders undermine
sand martin & vole
slipping where

feathered meadow grasses take flight
in flocks of green
presences slide into shadow

playground bully
is it? made coward crying mother
mother   the dark dazzles

slid presences   minds falling
under the set-piece advance
spat at by shrapnel from shell-cases set

in the set-piece English village
as vases set for daffodils
where children gather for harvest

and many a mother hopes
her unwell child be well
the night-winged terrors subside

as rooks glide
in the dawn
over bye-lane   bridle path

stook and crop-laden cart
won't chide too gently or too well
the children at the child's well

THE NECESSITY OF ICE

One frosted time
Orion rising roughshod
in a clenched & closing year

left us living meagerly   by coffee
cigarettes   by bread   alone
& wanting nothing more

than the slow tread of ice
too thin for any argument
from icecaps that are yesterday's news

will soon have no mysteries
to conceal or reveal
dwindling to the thinness

of a concave lens
focussing all our contraries
to diamond point of need

for the rigour & dispassion
of ice   its clarity & clouded mystery
its thermal equilibrium

We need its night-time crack & groan
of shifting darknesses
floe & crevasse   berg & glacier

& structures that are given to us to name
We need so much light
so many cool rooms   & music

we need icebergs to see the tip of
ice to pack against pain
to cut with others

to put our plans on   or to crush
with lemon & vodka   & melt
in warm young mouths

THE INSCRUTABLE SURFACE

If the sea rakes and scatters
long enough,
they may crack

revealing beneath
their inscrutable surface
ammonite, frond, shell

each one impressed
by what it seems to hold
balanced and weighed

and sent with a flick to skim
like a real stone
the surface of meaning

THE WINDOW

Words perch at the edge of dream
& if they scatter like gulls
disturbing the morning

will you rise to greet them
& the heralded journey
into life's sweet commotion

whose crash & surge shredded
through the ear's filter fractures
like sunlight on sea

sea on rocks   rocks
ground to sand   sifted
through the pin-prick neck of time?

The window overlooks the sea
Which is it to be?
Bow-wave & salt spray   the many voices

or the silence of the morning sky
whose light extends
its unseen invitations

Out of sight
out of mind's compass
beyond the waking households

work-worn
work-shy
burdened & light of soul

beyond the waves' whispered persuasion
the early   clear light
that coaxes the circling gulls to quiet

LYING TOGETHER

Lying together we touch
fine skin & hair soft
as ships' calls on the fog-bound river
of my early days
of tidal surge
that bleeds both youth & age.

Lying together we touch
wood that all be well & the bairns
between us take their parts
& grow timely into them
as we have into those
we could not but choose

Lying together we touch
the searching tongues
of yesterday that curl their flesh
to tell us in uncertain terms
that the gentle battles of the night
are over when we choose defeat.

LIKE LAPWINGS

The pair of lapwings you point out
Dance over fells in cloudy light

Clasp contour, angle wings
As over all misgivings

The winds of chance will turn me;
The paradigm of our breathless journey

Over lake & ridge
Praxis & sudden knowledge

Mend us as the day mends;
Sunshine, & the breeze sends

Wavelets over the dark lake,
Reflecting, when clouds break

The clear fells where lapwings fly,
Between them, it seems, telepathy.

COLD

He was no relation,
but closest kin, and cold,
appearing in places
known to me, but paled,
as things are paled by passage,
cryptically, and wild.
Skies can tell us much
they say, and earth contains
all the songs and stories.
When some will come, or won't
or insist on coming
only at night, only
in dreams, then that's a sign.
The shifting stair can cause
disequilibrium, and bring
footsteps at dawn, by windows
open to allow
the cooling breeze, the scent
of morning, the sound
of cars, of trees, a passer-by,
no relation, but closest
kin, and wild, seen
in places, streets, in fields
known to me, and wild.

A STONE

for Eloïse

… let me tell you
about a small girl I remember;
see her, stock-still, as she kept
her distance from the other lives.

She didn't join in, that morning,
with those who played in the trees
to multiply the universe,
nor did she run across the beach
towards yet more light.
But look, she has continued
on her path to the bottom of the dune—
footprints prove it threading
between thistles and sea.

And close to them, you can make out
the broader tracks
of a companion,
his prints filling with water
that doubles the sky.

(after Yves Bonnefoy)

A LULL

You may hear it
on the air waves,
or the sea breeze at night,
from a car radio
or someone's open window,
    as I heard it
in a pub garden one June evening
watching carefully for pipistrelles in the dusk
as a snatch of melody or beat
directing my feet
to The Sunny Side of the Street
or telling me I Shall Be Released.

You may see it point
to where spring blossom whitens woods
like the first grey in a man's beard.

You may hear it ask forgiveness
plead insanity
refuse to stand trial;
null and void in legal terms
yet still able
to bring bats in the dusk,
memories of night,
the music of touch.

You may feel
that it makes a pub garden
on a June evening
seem a sea calmed,
a port gained,

a shelter shared,
a welcome
a call
a lull

On the edge of the estate there were fields that stretched as far as the Cheviots; snow-capped even in a warm spring. A pond with creatures you could catch in nets. A tree bending over it like a woman washing her hair. Sodium lights all night, the attentions of the police, cold.

But acceptably cold because it was always someone else who shivered. It was, he said, like living in another person's past, and then you see the child outgrow you, and become someone you once knew but who never knew you After his mother died, it started. Resentments. Incompatible personalities. And on the road of good intentions a person may become intentionally homeless: if he deliberately does or fails to do anything in consequence of which he ceases to occupy accommodation which is available for his occupation.

Thus spake the Housing Act 1996.

& once a tree spread its green
over children, council houses
on the edge of the green belt
    of the green world
a pond with newts & frogspawn
where under, in, throughout,
    the tree's domain
an odyssey of nets & boots
    sought scents of other places
in defiance of what it knew

the sparrow's freedom
& the giggle of a small child
    swinging in its branches

under an evening expanse
empty only
    of all things
between the blue, white, orange stars
crisp as apples the frosty night reveals them
    configuring the darkness
with myths that cry out for belief

Childhood. Mother held it together. Like the roots of a tree. Roots on a crumbling bank. When you don't see someone, they become a memory only. The main elements of policy became law in 1985, the consensus being that, no single cause could be identified, as there were in fact a number of complex inter-related determinants. The agencies involved were charitable and full of good intentions, and Housing Benefit for 16-18 year olds was abolished.

With that temptation to Sloth and Avarice removed, the main elements of cold, hunger and your own invisibility couldn't prevent life on the street beckoning like the green country across the river. In a society which didn't exist, how easy it became to seek your fortune, as the novelty of tramps under the Embankment became a whole generation: a travelling nation going nowhere.

Lifestyle & Freedom
    to choose

gull-called estuary
    or shivered limestone spring

yesterday & today
    your lapping waters say

A tree reveals its roots
   where the bank crumbles
where new laws undermine
those without offspring
   or dependents
& no statutory right to a home
whom the road entreats you
   to rest in movement
like the wheeling gull
gone inland from gales
& salt swell
& long gone
   swirling green clouds
in the swirling waters
among the boots & nets
   a child's cry
tangled in the bows

Sunlight on a fountain
   pigeons scattering
statistics & complex
inter-related determinants
   & you
you could be anywhere
bobbing among unnumbered heads
in city squares

lost in the river of faces
the roots that sap
the mother's grip
the father's shaken tears
the lap of waves
the dream of rain

the city streets where you walk
blessed maybe by amnesia

Was it my mother? Or is it only me, remembering. Her hair.
Leaves. Nets trawling for newts all summer. I sleep when my eyes
get tired. I'm lucky enough to have a place to stay at the moment,
where I'm warm and welcome. I know it's morbid, but I keep a
little tally in my head of all my friends who've died on the streets.
He suddenly left the family home, telling them he would call them
the following day. No one in his family has heard from him since.
If you have seen him, or have any information, please call the
Helpline.

THE ELECTION CANDIDATES PROMISE
TO BE TOUGH ON THE CAUSES OF DISORDER

Car doors secured, fathers leave for their orderly office,
Mothers leave for school with their disorderly children

Sparrows seek asylum in the orderly sunlight,
Squabble for scraps in the disorderly breeze.

At the airport, a man is detained on suspicion of future disorder
By officers who assure him that Britain is an orderly place

Although the man is afraid of uniforms & order
& policemen, & soldiers drunk & disorderly

& is afraid of the locked room where he'll await a court order
Which may send him back to his country's civil disorder

In a van down the road that smacks of order,
Cars bound for the office, mothers & disorderly children.

BACK TO NEWCASTLE BLUES

i. m. Barry MacSweeney

'… it is altogether time
to nip under
the plover's wing and sleep …'

The work's unfinished
under wraps
& hung with signs saying

WARNING:
CONTAINS STRONG LANGUAGE
flexing poetry

to bend the bars
slip the chain-gang
lose the corporate bloodhounds

& find some delectable upland
free at last
on Tynedale fells

from B&Q
Sainsburys
& the Enterprise Zone

from a heritage
of law, linn and lough
& a dream of Silver Lonnen

betrayed
into moneyed elegance
in the cafés of Grey Street

& a born-again quayside
where Paddy's Market hawked
its ragamuffin merchandise.

SHIFT/CHANGE

Hark! Hark! The dogs do bark!

In the summer province
where the arched bridge parts the stream
toddlers plodge where swallows skim
& horses amble across at changes of shift,
expecting apples.

A thousand feet below
men on hunkers hack at coal.

The beggars are coming to town.

mobhanded from rigs and contracts
blasted building sites-
cum-airy-palaces

shiftless & shifted
out of joy-ridden villages
where a calligraphy of seams

writes off land
as reclaimed waste

& one in a velvet gown ...

going over the hill
to lay his burden down
as the bluesman sang

out loud to see them,
scattered, drifting,
on the backs of horses run wild.

ONCE IN WESTERHOPE WORKINGMEN'S CLUB

much overtime & double-time was spent
in crisp notes, straight from the shift spent
scaling the sides of precarious ships.
Deal cards, order pints, bottles of broon,
twenty tabs & a box of dominoes,
& one for yoursel bonny lad.
I supped it clearing smoke-wreathed
tables glass-stacked delicate replica
steelworks (long closed) seeing
welders, platers, fitters, apprentices
& bow-legged Walters and Arthurs
once rickety children bent by labour, hearing
the barmaid scolding 'there's no need for language'
as if there wasn't need for language to ask

what were they doing those hard-handed men,
drinking and playing dominoes
in the shadow of shipyards soon to be gone?
Didn't they know that time would come
no demarcation dispute could hold up,
no work-to-rule could win concessions from?

They did, as do we all. & yet
they loitered with intent
to drink their inexorable fill
& offer up each brokered advantage
to the drift of the river that ushered their ships
towards the past,
to the barmaid calling time, to the overtime
& the double-time spent scaling
those unsinkable ships.

THE STRANGE CITY

TRAJECTORIES

Arriving by bus in a strange city

Waking in a room
with open curtains
on an indeterminate day

Rooftops gleam in morning light
like difficult decisions

A zone of newly-constructed space
through which adjacent lives might glimpse
a primary school class in 1966
round the piano, singing
'Drink to me only with thine eyes'

Jove's nectar must have been
what my father drank
in brown bottles by the fire and telly,
a tiny silhouette of the Tyne Bridge
on its label

*

The strange city
becomes accustomed to my eyes,
its trajectory of optimism
takes me to political theory
and the price of coffee in Derby,
where the railways lurk
like Banquo's ghost
at the feast
of business parks
link roads, junctions
airport runways

And I heard it on TV
after the Hatfield train crash:
The head of the rail network
emerging from a meeting with fellow directors to tell the press:
'we've been thinking unthinkable thoughts'

*

Fox droppings, fleece on fenceposts,
beyond the field, in mist,
a road hums
with unanswerable knowledge
and bids us to be on our way
while it attends to
encroaching cigarette butts
and men with tape measures

The attitudes of harm
are omnipresent,
life as a series of events, some connected,
and the world a theory, waiting to be proved.

But let's get on with it you say:

your life
    or lives
from 'collateral damage: the movie'
to lists of Jews
to the evening news
and Bethlehem under siege
    a front-door shuts
a car passes, a kettle is filled,
conversation downstairs
and outside the window
tree-lined boulevards lead into spring

advancing sunlight reflects
a rise in the Dow Jones
0% finance
and everything Made in China

*

Speak to me only with thine eyes
thy lips, thy tongue, thy body
and that voice

I need that voice
like the world needs love

faced with CO_2 emissions
and rising seas
I need
a kiss
a cup
and some kind of nectar

*

Forgotten hopes sidle up
like homeless people
we spare some change for

How long will it be like this?
the ratios of empowerment
bending the odds
spring sunlight jamming the frequencies
air everywhere fair, or might be
And I was there
when the leather struck the netting
like a speculator opening an account

a blow-by-blow account
of how the world was won
to roars of 'Howay the lads'
as the crowd pours out of the ground
(so many, I had not thought Sunderland had undone so many)
scarves against the cold, beery breath,
winter lights on the ferry
where latecomers watch replays of missed penalties
ghosts of keelboats haul their coal,
and the Captains of Industry think unthinkable thoughts

*

Along the line of the valley
between Castle Rock and the Trent:
the railway, canal, factories,
once lacework, female labour,
depots and offices designed,
in the seventies
blues clubs and reggae,
and from this vantage
hindsight underestimates

*

Early evening
cannabis smoke drifts above the festival
stagestruck songbirds singing in the dimness
and the world is full of children,
some of them grey-haired and stooping

big drag, and then it happened,
the road shining, trees bowing as we passed:

the new Mazda 20v 1.8ltr 4WD with sunroof

because you care about your car

*

I like the way you walk

I like the way you walk
into my life
each day
like someone else's taste in music
    their radio playing
    'My Baby Wrote Me a Letter'
despatched by night mail
to a dawn platform,
where passenger trains arrive
at a world full of children
    each contigent
    upon each other
or so the language can say
in its brighter moments
among the jingles and slogans
realised as what words are for

If you drink to me only with those eyes
    I'll take the pledge with mine
O quench that thirst
    it's from soul, heart and soul

Get me a ticket for an aeroplane
    an intercity bus, a fast train

*

Out across the Midlands, low hills
motorways and lines of pylons, the airport
and its destinations, hitchikers at the junction
collateral and contingent,
their questions worn like new clothes
doled out to Jarrow marchers

Egg and sausage at the truckers café,
strong tea and we're ready to set out

NEXT, PLEASE

It seems like only yesterday, but already it's today;
feeling my way across the car park to a place in the sun,
learning the ABCs of self-reliance and signing up to the charter
guaranteeing safe passage through suburbia
while summers accumulate a residue of events
like queuing for the bathroom while the clock ticks across the hall
through the dining room and out over the lawn
to early morning liquid call of house martins, circling.
Listen to their calls, brought all the way from southern Africa.
What do they mean? The TV in another room explains
the structure of DNA or how to boil an egg. Listen
to those competing dialects, try them for free,
not one of them remains what it was yesterday.
We are what we say we are, and sometimes not;
because even pine kitchens and Everybody
Loves a Bargain can underplay the weather
and the operations of Fate. I think about this as I watch the martins
unwind the summer with studied imprecision, while the sky,
empty of tables and wine glasses, presents an unambivalent blue,
a ghost of blue, ambivalence of wings, song of morning,
The Most Moving Thing You'll Hear This Summer.
Sans serif and a little jaded, the alphabet declines to take
the long haul to green language, opting instead to speak
only of what it knows: views over the wooded valley,
and settlements down there, among the passing thoughts,
where words fall in an intellectual autumn, a swirl of constructed life.

ALL AROUND US

Who will speak for the birds? They have no language of their own,
flung here and there by windy air, and ignorant of charts,
as if low-pressure systems grew on trees, which of course,
they don't, at least not that I'm aware. Weather-vanes tell you nothing;
keep catalogues of laundry, you never know whether old receipts
and specious love-letters might redeem a wilting life.
All around us, the galaxies—eyes that are naked alone cannot see them.
Give me my escallope shell of quiet, turn on the bathroom light
I think there's a spider in here of immense proportions.
I'm interrupting this semi-permanent hiatus to note that Baroque pearls
are pearls with no definite shape. They are simply oddballs.
Bla bla bla I never update bla bla bla I suck, yeah I know.
April is like, cruel or whatever. Finlay seemed far away.
You can't read the signage at Little Sparta from those heights.

JOSEPH WRIGHT

A lamp in a darkened room
picks out a folk memory

I know where the mills were,
and the ironworks, the union banners,
a river that runs underground now,
the labour of children

*

Tax concessions and flexible labour
open up this town. The world is waiting,
crowded into Cromford Mills:
building workers from Poland and Croatia,
maids from the Philippines, competitive rates of pay.

Open up this town.

Arkwright, trailing smoke and sparks,
steps into Arcadia with engines and workers,
mills and ironworks, incidental light

*

Mechanics of perception,
a white canvas, ghosts
stalking the geographical wonders,
the great coaching inns fetching trade
along the routes of industry,
a Grand National Trades Union
a layered perception flowing underground
science of hope, mechanics
of a new society.

Somewhere, the notion of a better life,
a river, a town, its ghosts,
a geography of common wealth,
if we could only find it.

I had a notion that
layered experience lay in this town,
lamp in a darkened room.

*

A notion of light
and mechanics of perception,
layered geography, ghosts
of past masters, open up a route
through the Derwent valley,
past the mills and forges
to landscapes of feeling,
alchemy of craft and enlightened views.
Under a dark outcrop an earthstopper
works by lamplight.
In the library of a great house
a philosopher is giving 'that lecture on the Orrery
in which a lamp is put in place of the Sun'
to work the motion
of light, swaying
through the minds of the people,
and gravity, in perfect balance,
energy, to pump the mills,
coal, smoke, sparks
strange machines in the lit air
of Derby's workshops, in place
of handwork 'these cotton mills, seven
stories high and filled
with inhabitants, remind me

of a first-rate man of war,
and when they are lighted up
on a dark night look
most luminously beautiful'

*

Cars cross St. Mary's Bridge, office workers
lie in the sun at lunchtime, the mill
inhabits a silence, two girls
are dazzled by an ingot's glow

The crags of Derbyshire darken,
landowners pose for portraits, and the friends
of a young artist, his writers and poets,
are young still, in perfect balance,
with gravity, mechanics, the construction
of strange machines
out of canvas and painted light,
most luminously beautiful,
first-rate, and filled with inhabitants.

(REPRISE)

Arriving out across the Midlands,
tacking windblown

eyes on the road, hands on a wheel
mind on something, a notion

that in this town layers
can be revived, at least that common aim

once thought beautiful in early evening
Castle Rock, the Trent

blues clubs and seventies reggae,
lacework, female labour

railway, canal, factories
a sight once held most magnificent

it might be said, to undercut works
of hands, forgotten

hopes, sidling acquaintance
with layers of

up-to-the-minute and waiting to be lived,
out across the land, tacking

to a common aim, Arcadia by lamplight
a common hope across the years.

THE WORLD SEEN FROM THE AIR

THE CONDITIONS

... or where they came ashore, they say,
looking lost, but hopeful

to strains of music, their new life
wild fruit, campfires, nightfall

with low cloud, a trail of white
behind a ship, a sense of not belonging

and time, a disc reflected in the sea, children
making a racket and birds nesting on the rocks,

ask, is this all there is, yes,
happenings with low cloud, a sense

of time, reflected, nests on ledges
and overwhelming, so small these happenings

a long trail of white, I used to
be so free, the time so rich

on a shoreline lit and full of time
happening to those present without will

just happening   just like
and if it were evenly spread, but time

and all its tales stands tall among us
the birds making a racket, the children

asleep in our houses
with totally unjustified absolute trust

as if a disc in sea's light
reflected in eccentric circles

statements of intent whose reflections
quiver all directions out

a disc in sea's light, low cloud, trail of white,
a sense of not belonging

and these are the conditions
as we see it, pertain to us

the waters wait the children wait
the shore waits, a disc

in sky's light, reflected in the eaves
so small these happenings

the waters' cool draws a breath
in each one, a breathless rhythm

that pertains to us and to the world
so world pertains to us

rhythm and breath is part of that
attuned to rhythm and aware

of this memory and the next   a part of breath
and a rhythm of attention   a part of world

and a rhythm of remembering   children we see
swimming close to shore

and everything's imagination except the waves' cold
close of water and the rhythm swimming requires

past shallows into swell   lights
and welcome foothold   dark shore

hanging on a word
as breathless and attuned attention

breath and presence
rhythm and time

living requires
breath and memory

rhythm of waves
rhythm of youth

and another shore to get to
things made up

imagination playing tricks
past shallows, into swell

dark shore, lights
and welcome foothold

VARIATIONS ON PAINTING A ROOM

in late winter/early spring, lilac
emulsion spreading like a curious mind,
watching the trees outside

while sipping a glass of Coke,
(for Coke adds life)
and pondering the quote
on a scrap of newspaper:
'religion used to be regarded
as the opium of the people, now
drugs are that opium'

reflecting on how
the world walks, then runs

in a poem about
being rain-washed, sun-dried,
stunned by the claims of affection
alone in a house
on an early spring day
watching the trees outside
painting a room lilac

watching the trees
thinking that life is the opium of the people
hoping the trees
might re-invent my mind
as process/wind/air/light

    +++

or a poem called:

I Painted my Room in a Colour Named Lilac

in which the world walks
    then runs
(air/light)
as a process of verb
to imagine a single heartbeat
is a process of speech,
    process of energy,
to invent, re-invent
     a few remaining
trees outside a lilac room
lilac outside a curious mind
outside a process of air and light

thinking that
is the religion
of the intelligent
the opiate of the rain-washed
sun-driven experience
of an early spring day,
alone in a house

dazzled by the process, music,
a book of hours, open

to the process of wind/air/
lightly chosen, in a life

carried off the scale, notes on the
fall of a sparrow, so many notes

played in a dazzling scale
to those remaining

curious and curiouser, at last
stunned, by claims not made by us
of affection, of speech,
of naming, outside the lilac room

the parts of speech
known to us

as houses, rented rooms
in a Midlands hung-over and dazzled

leaves like copper, lilac
or at least something called
back from the brink of forgetting
timely,
    and fraught with distance

    +++

a poem about

the Midlands, a life of flats and rented houses,
hangovers dazzled by copper leaves
in post-industrial sunlight

music, and minor variations
on life,
a book of hours,
open on the page of now,
inscribed with every sparrow's fall,
pasted with lilac emulsion,
stunned by the claims of affection,
alone in a house
on an early spring day,
watching the trees outside

painting a room lilac

+++

the poem says
we are verb, conjunction
        and part of speech

a force nine gale
driven into a single heartbeat

+++

is this a poem

painting a room

or reading a newspaper again

'William Hill does take bets
on the Second Coming,
(odds at 1,000:1, though
for this confirmation is needed
from the Archbishop of Canterbury)'

and is it now about
taking bets?

on a sparrow's fall
or the chances
    of being stunned
into a conjunction
    of memories come again
    at such long odds

curious emulsion spreading
like trees outside my mind
inside the room
on a spring day,
claimed, like unlikely winnings
as a process of hope

+++

… or, to put it another way,

variations
on a book of years
inscribed with the odds
on the Second Coming
   of a lilac room
on a lilac day
and a curious mind
stunned into leaf
by the claims of process
and the opening of the bar
across the lilac road

and from the bar, the poem suggests
might come music, a song
I listened to once,
called 'waiting for the end of the world'
that might have been
a song I heard

that might have been
suggested by the process of imagining
how the world turns
into a process of remembering
and being remembered

+++

The Poem Called
  when I was doing something else

it may have been spreading
emulsion
        like lilacs
or memories of The Potteries'
bottle kilns, or rows of terraced houses

or a curious mind
that reinvents
  a room, lilac, a spring day
and a poem about
  a lilac room
and a day in season

watching the trees outside
and the bar across the road
open its doors
this day in early spring

watching the trees outside, thinking that
watching the trees
is thinking about saying that
the trees might re-invent themselves

as my mind invents a room, in lilac
distant and fraught
and brought back
to the claims of affection

and the way the world runs,
on an early spring day,

on a day, early in lilac,
on an early lilac day, in spring

THE WORLD SEEN FROM THE AIR

To get used to the earth's edge
and pale vertigo is   to lose

something not altogether   but
the lights at night each little spark

and fugitive energy the evening sees
the cars like living things turned fossil

to fuel the night's decline the day's
displaced indifference

dusk, and the aircraft stack like geese
coasting in to land on a thawed lake   the snows

no longer, is a learned indifference, rather
an acceptance of the spread plains, the sea's

inscrutability, the cities studded
as far as we can see

(there's nowhere to rest my notebook)

to get used to the earth's pale edge
is something not altogether lost   as

(there's no where to rest)
it lights each little spark and fugitive energy

the evening sees the cars see
the living things turned fossil

to fuel the night's decline the day's indifference
dusk, and the aircraft stack like geese

the snows a learned indifference, rather
an acceptance as far as we can see

(there's nowhere to rest this ...)

*

what is between us
    is lacking certainty,
the bowl of sleep
    at least of
time shared, time imagined

leaves in the breeze and the glare
of a hazy day, churn of cold water
        guillemots, gannets,
nests, ledges in the glare of sea,
and others
        between us flight
    a swift sleeps
    on the wing

a bowl shared, time shared
flight imagined at the borders
 and churn of ledges, rocks
in the glare of sealight

we have come this distance,
inland, a sparrow's flight,

a swift sleeps on the wind,
the air as earth to us, the earth

alien, and peopled with the strange,
incapable of speed and movement

or rest, and sky will enter in
our eyes, the wind our ears

as if we could master it only in
stillness, and that at best

or sky that will enter in
our eyes, and wind our teacher

the leaves in the haze of day,
cold water, breeze, a bowl

might mitigate the time spent
or imagined between us, sleep

a swift on the wing, or rest
might mitigate the cold

of earth, as alien, we have come
this distance, a sparrow's flight

peopled with the strange, leaves,
cold water, churning flight

*

Memory extends its current
in the late air,
different shades for different
depths and directions

sedge, willow and alder, a pair of kingfishers,
blue jewels, quick,
sedge, willow and alder, a pair of blue jewels
like kingfishers your eyes

blow the wind southerly

*

a studied velocity
and wing flick
    turns a line to lift
these birds never alight
a life on the wing

and a perspective on life
all summer weave and call
feed nest
    from this vantage point the town and lake

the summer migrants and the herons
with the slow wing-beats
  enclose

wherever humanly possible, an image
of the lilies of the field

(I should have been a bird)

the children lulled to sleep by their calls
their wills weakened, letting slip
the calls of evening

each leavetaking like the last, to rest,
migrants calling time on summer

wherever possible the practice will
continue, they are exemplars, some will say

wing-flick and slow beat, migrations
and sedentary populations

spread across the surface of the globe,
in transience, lulled to sleep, or woken

the calls of the evening and the weave
of feeding, nesting, wave on wave

To leave your home and know
there's no returning

so many suffer such a fate,
so many lulled to sleep,

perspective on life awake, right here, now,
no time to waste or weaken

*

(midnight)
each little spark and fugitive energy
the cars see the living things turned fossil

to fuel the night's decline, the day's
and the aircraft stacked like geese

the snows gone and a learned indifference,
rather an acceptance

*

Tracery of branches
brushed by south wind

A heron makes the sky a home

In continuous brush-stroke light
I cast my mind across a pool of answers
we may go fishing later

*

Sedge and willow, alder, a pair of eyes
blue jewels, quick kingfishers,
a pair of blue jewels
sedge, willow and alder, your eyes

and a wind in the sedge

*

As if it were
    brush strokes
or streaks of cloud half-visible
in what we call vision
    but now know better ...

as mind bends to perspectives,
brush strokes, sleep, slowly
to the hum of engines, the
earth, I take it, tentative, and
encompassed by sleep,
a vision of sorts

yet streaks of cloud known better
than the hum of engines
we need to talk, she said,
as the brush of sleep stroked

encompassed the bending vision
  seas, the open shore, night

earth, I take it, tentative, and
encompassed by a vision of sorts

MEANDERS

An ordinary day, speaking through
its ordinary creatures

that water's song and time of year
for starting out, green and its shades

sand martins nesting in burrows
on the far bank, call and curl

move as a group to the river's surface,
becoming hard to see in reflected glare,

as if they know that to scratch
the surface of liquid

is to enter a world of transition,
a natural system, tending to stasis

as the rotation (some say) of the Earth,
here undercuts sediment

lets sand martins nest in burrows on the far bank,
move together through the ordinary day

*

as if to call and curl, to scratch,
reflect, as if to surface
    in a world
is imprinted on its form, variations
of current, slope,
    and the ordinary rotation

of a day   speaking   a surface

*

the singing (some say) of the Earth

*

the hungry bird, the never still bird

the trees, the cumulus, the blue sky

the relentless hunter bird and its insect prey

are following a meandering path

    on an ordinary day
    in the air-conditioned office

a day when world leaders are meeting

a day when nothing in particular takes place

a day with you and me

imprinted on its form, of variations

in current, slope,

    and ordinary rotation

a day of call and curl
a day of hunger, never still

*

is it the rotation of an ordinary day?
or the day of a poem sloping

through call and cumulus, through expressions
of surface and song, that water's

form of words, meeting
of world and world, variations

on a form of hunger, as nothing
takes place, relentlessly, nothing

is ordinary, and takes place from
a privileged vantage, from green

of transition to water's song
and time of year for starting out

A SEPARATE BREEZE

A place to be
    like no other
by the unpaved track and the poplar
  a dance of leaves
  a sound of surf
you have to let life happen
  an agency
and passage clear between islands
  so close you could touch
  a presence in the early hours
lying awake until you hear the latch

over miles of sea
  another country
  where the children live
a separate breeze in the leaves
a route taken, or not
it doesn't matter
    life happens

open to the elements
    all year round
rock strata, a geology, untold
time passing between us,
  the current, silted,
  leaves a narrow channel,
most of the broad straits unnavigable

Mind how you go on the path
So quiet the house

A good crop on the apple tree this year,
wasp and snail under October skies
  start of term,
  they say you get used to it,

the sound of waves on estuary shores
    the headland clear

The sea turns below the sliced cliff
strata curved by processes

open to the imagination
over so long perfected so long

a plot and genealogy, such as we have
when we walk the tide-line

on a last family holiday, snapshots
and diary entries, flux and process

of imagination strata exposed
feelings exposed quiet exposed

house all year round, a place
like no other, between islands

and a sea outside, I listen to
lying awake to hear the latch

*

Look I said, if you lie on the grass out here
you can see the Milky Way
    Rolled their eyes and smiled at each other
    but came anyway

heard sea-surf sounding below the cliff
    at dawn the tides withdraw, currents
        pull round the headland
        to the grey Atlantic

past Lundy Island, where seals stare
   like the souls of the drowned

*

a game of Monopoly while the rain drummed
on the caravan roof

and when it stopped, the deserted beach all ours
at low tide like a deserted planet

green-fringed, waterfalls onto shingle
headland after headland

seals like souls, tidal race
currents pull under sun

or milky way
calm or squall

seals in the tidal race
where we would flounder

an untold genealogy
passes between us

you wonder with a start sometimes
whether they still look the same

and what they're doing
right now, at this moment

under different skies
plying trades, busy

with the process of life, the passage
clear, the routes they took

harbouring or letting go,
and all the time

process of wind,
water, process of change

tides and cliff, a collection of shells,
a lost sandal, the making up of memory

from a series, diary entries, snapshots,
listen old man, she might say

life happens, out there across straits,
listening between islands

process of change
sound of waves and a sliced cliff

revealing a plot and family connection,
a route back to where the children were

taken or not, with all its consequences,
process and erosion, lying awake to hear them

HOTEL FEBRUARY

Not only are the internal organs vital, but dressing-gowns assume a new significance. A window which we didn't think was there has been opened especially for us, and what views it affords! Exquisite autumn colours, sun, clouds, the traffic jam on the bridge, the construction site. I'll take it all. The very thing itself is what it seems. Birds are involved, somewhere, ruffling the picture. The procedure is routine sir, 1000:1 chance of cardiac arrest, stroke or departing soul, and involves catheterisation of contingent reality and a transformational rebirth. It only takes ten minutes. Painless, if psychologically discomfiting. Your relatives will never seem so useful again, but dreams of spring may spontaneously erupt. Accept them, like the tears of your loved ones; they act as healing balm.

*

Walk slowly. Treat each step as if it were a child that must be brought into being with great pain, but, paradoxically, with love. It's progress. I'm weathered like a plank left out in the open, seasoned at last and ready to make a useful contribution to the future of the world. Barcodes make no more sense than they did. The wind is so much restless energy. Heere, about mine herte. The house opens its windows and yawns with delight across the park, even though the trees are rudely naked, disporting for my pleasure in an adolescent fashion. But it isn't me. There are many books to be read, movies to be watched, unholy rows with relatives to be had, and so little time, and I feel that if only orchestras discouraged whistling in the ranks, a sense of order might be restored.

*

3.10am. Breathe in. Breathe out. Outside, footfalls. Outside thick fog. The heart of the night. The foggy, blurred, sinister, confusing, damp, obbfuscating, chilly, familiar heart.

Of the night. Footfalls. Breath. The rhythm of pulse, of breath. There's no escape, no entry, no stopping, no retreat. Extensive tests/plenty of rest/the heart's beat/no retreat/breath, speech/a sudden breach. Dreams are an empty mirror. I must add new items to tomorrow's list: 1. Breathe in. 2. Breathe out. 3. Repeat indefinitely.

3.35am. The fog is still there. It has filled the previous twenty-five minutes. I understand at a profound level the irreducible essence of fog.

*

Mail arrives haphazardly, 8am, 5pm or not at all. Two Christmas cards, a book *Healing Into Life and Death* (early Xmas Present), a tax reminder, and a leaflet *Four Cases We Need to Highlight*. Following his arrest in October 2003, Reverend Samba was sent to one of Equatorial Guinea's most notorious prisons. And yet he has been charged with no crime and has had no trial. The Reverend Samba suffers from several chronic ailments, but the prison where he is currently held will not provide the treatment he needs ... He must rely on his family ... they can only visit a few times a year. A postcard with a picture of 'The Medicine Buddha (Skt. Baishajyagura; Tib. Sangye Menla) ... employed to remove all afflictions of body, speech and mind'.

*

Today, snow. Or rather, a memory of snow. In fact, fog. The TV sits up and begs for attention. It wags its tail and demands to be watched. If you repeat something often enough it becomes a form of truth, or at least a form of falsehood, or maybe neither but perhaps something you cease to question. That could be helpful. This is a chance to live in the present moment. This is a chance to live in the present moment. Not all emotions are red carpet events.

Not all empathy is real. Today's newspaper: Microchips in our brains and bodies will freeze the ageing process and ensure that everyone will be at the frontier of knowledge.

*

On the road to recovery! The Tin Man and his companions. The world was all before him and other literary references. Eat, drink, jog, swim, lift, swell, stretch. Entreat life-companions to be mutually available and counter-supportive. They'll be waiting. The boardroom has been booked. It is a glass room on the 30th floor overlooking the harbour with its refinery and dockyard. There'll be a room-full of people, hearts a-flutter, looking askance, nursing burning questions, hearts at ease, hearts recently electrocardiographed. I will need answers. Will you require an Electron Beam Tomography Scan? Electrophysiological testing? Are you the possessor of a Left Ventricular assist device? Do you have creases in your earlobes? Can you prise the lid off a jar of jam? Remove a spider from the bath? We hope you will still be able to fulfil your married duties. Are you still a caring father? Good. We will be in touch. Should we require your services we shall contact the agency. Goodbye.

FEBRUARY HOTEL

The migration exercise
has started, over continents
and seas, birds and others
have left for the season.
Hemispheres collide
with promise of work
at Calais, Heathrow,
Malta—boatlands from Africa
fetched up on its sands
The Virtual Private Network
is established. I work late,
phone home,
watch the moon rise over the city,
drink some Restore (Ideal After Meals)
and sink into a bed
shaped like a wish.
Outside the air is heart-shaped and empty.
The logic is conditional, circuitous,
airstreams are predictable,
year in, out over
continents and seas.
It is promise of work,
long journeys under cover.
The time elapsed is serial,
day and night encrypted, venal.
At last, the firewall is configured,
required ports opened
to outside traffic.
I work late,
phone home,
watch the moon risen
that can't stay long
over continents and seas.
Rachel is in Germany,

I'm on the road,
Rose and the youngest
home alone.
'Instructions for living'
might include
drink peppermint tea,
clean your teeth daily,
remember to tell her
'here is my life,
take it, it's yours.'
The big picture
that's the truth,
goods and services,
conditional logic,
the world reduced
to roads and airports.

TODAY THE SNOW

Today the snow, and tonight
it lies on my car, and on all
the roads that she must go.
To be in a warm hotel in midwinter,
isn't that enough comfort?
Today the snow, tomorrow
I will save you from the rest of your life,
or is it mine? I would like
to help someone to live after my death—
eyes, liver, kidneys, pancreas
left on the fields of morning
while I'm in a dreamless sleep.
What could be more idyllic
than an exhibition
of the latest luggage?
Are your shoes clean, young man?
One believes so. And who are we?
To argue, that is.
I earn a living, recount
colourful episodes from my past,
swell my feet on crystals of white.
Isn't that enough? But no.
'Our researches must continue'
and there are language courses
yet to be complete. The latest
adult films to be watched.
Slide softly into the bed of white.
Protect the night, snow,
and don't allow yourself to be fooled.

LITTLE ELEGIES

clouds over the cooling towers,
prophecies bloom, the trains
take forever through the mists
and tea plantations

tomorrow we will be read
said the poet, filling
her glass with ballerinas and porcupine spines

*

the day drifted into the margin
and my words were left in the dark

*

a simple tale, told
on the simplest of days,
and yet, a morning more baffling than ever
ushers planet earth into view
and spins its children into hinterlands
that will carve their dreams
to the lonely shape of hope

*

a simple shape, a hope
sane and simple, shaped
by weariness of night
and clouds the hope of comfort

*

the plough, the twins,
the seven sisters ...

cloud banks and open skies

wandering worse for wear
towards home
enclosed in calm
and kept continually
under named skies
by friends and familiars
sleeping and wide awake

*

clouds bloom over the cool prophesies,
the trains are breaking out
into the mists
and simple plot constructions

a simple blooming
leading to
a simple hope of blooming

*

it's to the children the world goes,
their games and graces
they stand at the door of life,
each native to their place and peering
at an alphabet of sighs

*

astronomers have discovered
with gravitational microlensing
the most earth-like planet yet

'a frigid rock
orbiting a small star'

*

'this field is randomly drifting in time'
said the error report

*

as I discovered fields more strange
singing while I walked and baffled by
the acts of random time

night heaved at my eyelids

somewhere north by north-west
the pole star reigns,
the skies empty
into long nights
lit by walrus oil
and blinking radios

out there,
where poetry cannot follow

COMPLAINTS AND REASSURANCES

the beggar tugs at my sleeve
and I wonder, am I in a dream,
there are people in doorways
I can't quite see
'Ah, but they can see you'
said the doctor, fingering my pulse

the house under the moon
wants peace and tranquility
with a capital P and Q
but the pale evenings
whose hair floats 'like ebony'
continue, and I wonder if my doctor
really does believe my symptoms
they're so mild and courteous

he says I should think positively
of unexpected outcomes
but I think I should keep my eyes
on the ardent light low in the east
calm beyond incident
that offers neither hope nor comfort
as I lie awake longing for someone
not just anyone, the blue lake
and the mountains in snow—
the scene asks and answers
innocent and frail walk
with solemn dignity just out of earshot

the tugging at my sleeve continues—
the medical profession
isn't what it used to be,
like the night,
it offers no reassurance

but tells me instead that simple faith
is no longer a currency
accepted in any of its counting houses

THE MAN ACROSS THE PARK

It's 3.15 am.
Through my window I'm watching
a man across the park.
A winking light
across the park
signals to the night.
Across the park, houses.
The people in those houses,
their children,
what will happen to them?
A train sounds, then fades.
'Ye wretched of the earth'
someone should say.
The night sits impassively
on the world.
I would bring myself back
to where I am,
before the window of the dark,
in a sleeping house,
lucky for a while.
That print on my wall,
it's Hockney, *Lilies*,
lithograph on paper.
By the desk, A Bag for Life
in association with UNICEF.
That clock on my wall
its numbers are blurred.
There is a man
on a lit path across the park.
The longer I sit
the more he resembles me.
He is closer now
and looks in at me.
I'm not sure I recognise him,

but only tiredness,
the taste of coffee,
the feeling of being awake too long.
I might say that the world
is 'fleet of foot.'
The winds blow from all directions.
The car parks are full.
And if I sit till morning,
someone will stir,
the lilies, lithograph on paper,
will absorb the light.
The dogs across the park, their owners,
connected with the morning
and all the day's events
will sing as ever
of the wagging tail of happiness.
The man across the park
will be many people.

ENTER FISHERBOY, STAGE LEFT

Where are all the calls and emails? The desktop is crowded: luminous hardwood veneer, views of the outside world through a tinted window, a screen, the teeth of many pianos arranged in smiling majesty, a stack of technical manuals and an expenses form. May I take your credit card sir? Your room is of the best, with views of many previous lives, both your own and others. The estuary reflects its surroundings, allowing the refinery and the dockyard to impose their presence. Ships to other lands, far more remote than ours. And then the lives; this one in particular. Or was it a previous? A farm labourer in Lower Saxony circa 1700. Or a horse. Here are my things: laptop, mobile phone, clean shirt, bottle of elixir.

*

Am I mistaken, or do the officials in our quarter sidle like inept metaphors, disturbing the populace with dreams of fame? Across the railway bridge, lit up in the early dusk, the evening sings of thoughts that wrap themselves around places. Gypsy caravans on the stony waste ground, the target of many eyes, not always unhostile. We want them gone. We think our drives will be paved over while we sleep, and money demanded. We want them harried, evicted, fleeing, cleansed. 'Why not live and let live'? someone asks. The opening bars of many songs fail to answer. 'Can't we provide municipal facilities for them'? But rhetorical questions are not enough, and the blackbirds protest in song, innocent and free, although the worms are sceptical. A barefoot French fisherboy painted one hundred years ago by Augustus John holds his cap in supplication as if embarrassed by the sumptuous colours that surround him. The caravan-dwellers await a court order, knowing they have time.

*

These days my children and I are proficient dreamers, and have perfected our thinking skills to the point of no longer needing them. Once we swam in a mountain lake, cold in pale sunlight. The geese overhead lavished attention on the sky, and stirred in us strange feelings, not negative or vain. From the verandah we watched the rain fall in tropical quantities, as was the custom in those parts. Hello. Hello. I'd like room service. But no-one came except the pale children who avoided our gaze. The families on the dockside waved to their men as the big ship floated past.

*

The fisherboy would like to say something, but he is not even an original, only reproduced on a postcard propped up on my desk, waiting to be posted to a friend with a message apologising for non-attendance at a poetry reading. But let him speak anyway: 'The colours that surround me, that in fact are me, speak only of themselves, whereas I speak for the barefoot boy painted by the Englishman who stayed in our village in 1907. He (the boy) says he never saw the painting, only a rough sketch, and so, what can such art say about the worm's fear of the blackbird or the gypsyless opening bars of many songs? The colours of course can stand for anything or nothing at all, that is their tragedy and their …'

*

Across the bridge, in the dusk, not one person is that person. I would know her anywhere, even after all this time. Light on her feet, as before, and leaving me panting. My desk is too untidy. The telephone, the family photographs, the screen, papers, diary, these things are not indifferent. Stop screaming, all of you. Even you, reader. I type in /usr/bin/appservd, but in vain—the host machine is inaccessible.

85

The police paying a visit to the gypsies arrive in force. Across the bridge, the station impudently flaunts its departures in yellow LCD. The trains are crowded, the car park is said to be full. Lovers wave their handkerchiefs in Technicolour black-and-white, steam, the pain of parting. Yes, please, coffee with milk, number 72. Open to the world, I must be open to the world.

*

In winter, in these northern latitudes, night comes early, and the office is warm and lit, and hums with machinery and voices. The railway track is lit also, but the travellers' caravans are almost invisible. The management, in another country, take decisions in our interest. I have on my desk a Limited Edition pack of tomato ketchup (Heinz), a collection of rare paperweights, a postcard of *French Fisherboy* by Augustus John, and two theatre tickets for tonight's performance (run by the Ministry of Creative Arts). Ladies and Gentlemen, please take your seats. The page turns. It's the same one. Painted with sumptuous colours. Surely the sumptuousness of Life. 'Les couleurs ne sont qu'eux-mêmes'. True, mon ami, the colours are only themselves, and yet … Please sir, yes you. Step forward. The stage is lit. Applause ladies and gentlemen please. In the dark, the lit stage is its own world. The fisherboy enters stage left, then the gypsies with their tools and white vans. Right on cue, the Englishman, my children, inept metaphors and dreams of fame. The white hotel by the lakeside is silent. The geese are in the skies.

THE BOOK OF RANDOM ACCESS

The Book of Random Access has 64 sections, and each section has 256 words. 64 is the number of hexagrams in the *I Ching*, and both 64 and 256 are significant numbers in computing.

for John Bloomberg-Rissman

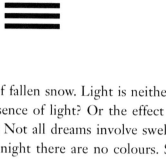

The texture and density of fallen snow. Light is neither a wave nor a particle, but the absence of light? Or the effect of light, tiny beautiful points of it. Not all dreams involve swelling and fruition, but some do. At night there are no colours. Stars are a monochrome, and I wish that, like them, I could be truly indifferent. The passage of time means that there are places I can never get back to—not that I want to, it's just that my going there is no longer under my control. In physics, time and space were considered fundamental quantities, therefore, the only definition possible was an operational one, in which time is defined by a series of periodic events. Perception of time arises out of the structure of the brain. Opposition arises from misconceptions. Either we misunderstand the Sage or Fate or the meaning of life, or the cosmic order of values, or ourself or others. If you lose your horse, do not run after it. Only yesterday, the blue sky (though streaked with aeroplane tracks) was over us as we walked through the grounds of Chatsworth House. The river ran over stones, and the sheep straggled the hill in lines, their feet crunching over the autumn leaves. Once we were pastoral nomads. But this isn't the Mongolian steppe. I have meetings to get to. Lines of sheep heading for fresh pastures over autumn leaves. I guess this could be considered serial music. I guess it could be considered a mosaic.

1.

Here, we have to contend with the sleeping world on its silent journey through space and car headlights circling. Doubt and fear cause us to split from our path. Take three pennies and drop them in a random fashion. Soon, the days will start to increase in length. The bright quality will be developed brighter and brighter from day to day, and month to month. Our faces are ugly and unpleasant, not because we are wearing a mask, but because we have lost the mask of youth. Driving through the Staffordshire countryside at night, with a full moon, we could see the fields outlined in silver, and the trees against the skyline forming a clear black border. This after a day at a theme park, a good day, the rides exhilarating, cold, clear autumn weather, surprisingly good tea and OK food. The adverts on Channel 5 go on a long time, and form a crass interlude to a documentary about a Jewish family who survived the Warsaw ghetto and were reunited against all odds at the end of the war. Withdrawal is the way the *I Ching* relates to our ego; it is the way we are meant to deal with the ego of others. As long as we are sincere, the *I Ching* relates to us. Forgetting aids orientation in time. Cases have been recorded of people who (by ordinary standards) forgot so little that their everyday activities were full of confusion. Thus, forgetting seems to serve the survival of the individual and the species.

Bless her. Phew! The stories in the papers are getting worse. Write to John, thanking him, and apologizing for not turning up the other night. Shopping: beer/fruit/oats/tea. Get a price for a new PC. Plan Birmingham trip. As long as we are preoccupied with the day-to-day, we can forget about the year-to-year. As long as we're preoccupied with the year-to-year ... in 1629 at the age of twenty-one, the apprentice poet wrote his first masterly poem, the Nativity Ode. From then on his life had a fixed purpose. I might perhaps leave something so written to aftertimes, as they should not willingly let it die. The Summer of Love. Flowers, daffodils they were, scattered on the seats of the concert hall, light shows during the gig. It was all so innocent in those days, before the big promoters took over. We made our way from the Tor, walking mostly, the wildflowers were so beautiful, the wind fresh. Memory, that's what we are, our lives, our identity, all made of memory. Try forgetting, then see what happens. It is more like stumbling into a clearing in the forest, where suddenly you can move and see clearly. To experience emptiness is to experience the shocking absence of what normally determines the sense of who you are and the kind of reality you inhabit. Like a lobster, emptiness might be something not to everyone's taste. Remember, when you wake, the shape of a wind-carved rock in a sandy landscape, its features looking like a face, wrinkled, without wisdom.

There are more numbers still to arrive, and yet, the valley is quiet, as if equations couldn't really solve our problems, and what came to a head in the days when light was soft and easier on the eye than the battered visage that the world wears now may be finally laid to rest. A meadow was a meadow, and on windy days the people would fly their kites in peace. People laughed out of turn. No-one feared the summer, each one raised his head confidently. The numbers added up. Numbers, text, pictures, audio, and nearly any other form of information can be converted into a string of bits, or binary digits, each of which has a value of 1 or 0. This is memory. Distributed among the cities of the world, the marginal lands available to the few remaining hunter-gatherers, in the personal effects of innumerable people, a continuing song, the lay of the great journey, collective and incomplete. Today is like wading into a pool not knowing the depth, but the cool is organized and molecular, like the rain occurring at a random place and seascape, rising, as if this place were a dream of this place, in space, where all the laws are different. A meeting at ten, lunch, missed the bus and walked all the way home, trying to concentrate on the present. Why try to concentrate on it? What else is there to be aware of? Your memories are all in the present, just as much as those trees over there.

4.

Some days, words are as slippery as an eel, as mysterious as the mind of a fish. Some days there is mist and scenery, strange birds. Some days I'd like to take notes on ornithology, study the flora to help me make a home. Some days, the world seems remote. That's a plain way of putting it. Not all strings lead to a labyrinth, but many do. That's another way. The ruins of Minos' palace at Knossos have been found, but the labyrinth has not. The enormous number of rooms, staircases and corridors in the palace has led archaeologists to believe that the palace itself was the source of the labyrinth myth. They lived in a maze of tenements and courtyards around Sandgate, near the Tyne and the Ouseburn. Parents, six children, Grandma, all in two rooms. Twelve families in the courtyard, the bairns all played together. So long ago, and not many of them left. He liked to dress in his Sunday best. When he was working, me mother wad send iz tae the pawnshop on Sat'dae. She'd say, here's half a croon, gan an get yor faather's suit. Drumrolls and a marching band. As aa came from Sandgate aa hord a lassie sing. I look at a photograph, a street scene from the early twentieth century, and find it strange to think that everyone in the picture is now dead. I sometimes reflect on that when walking through a shopping mall in Derby or Nottingham. The subtle thief of youth (that's hard to say).

[It] is the recording of people's memories. It is the living history of everyone's unique life experiences. They have created our fate. To try to change this fate by wrestling with it or resisting it, is to tread on the tiger's tail. But there are no tigers round here, just dogs. I see them across the park in the brittle winter sunshine, cavorting with their kind and ignoring their owners' instructions. It could be worse: after all, the only expectations of a dog are to eat, and sleep, and perform other bodily functions, and sometimes go for walks and wag its tail, or splash into a muddy river after a stick. But why? The unexamined life is not worth living. The taming power of the small. Our life is limited by circumstances. The ninth hexagram, second line: he allows himself to be drawn into returning. I was eleven when I started work for a shoe-maker, helping in the workshop of a night from school, knocking clog bottoms off, knocking nails out of hob-nailed boots after the shop shut at night, and they used to keep open until eight o'clock every night as long as there was a customer; if there was customers coming in they would stay open until ten. Across the park, the dogs run free, one might say heedless, in the sunshine. Do not serve mean ends. Do not live in unawareness. Do not embrace false views. Do not be a world-upholder. I have to go; there's something I want to watch on TV.

Sanitise your shoes here! Lightweight scooters to fit in the boot of your car. You'll love our Halloween trick-or-treat bag. [Modern] folkloric evidence [may not] reflect how the holiday might have changed; these rituals may not be 'authentic' or 'timeless' examples of pre-industrial times. Halloween was perceived as the night during which the division between the world of the living and the otherworld was blurred, so spirits of the dead and inhabitants from the underworld were able to walk free on the earth. The tang of coffee, the cold, bright morning air, makes you feel alive. Dazzling sun on car windows on the A52. I feel good, I knew that I would now. James Brown is dead. The A52 is gridlocked. Counting the cars on the New Jersey Turnpike, they've all come to look for America. They've come to sanitise their shoes, to buy new scooters, to look for England. I see the girls walk by dressed in their summer clothes. Resonant rumour of sun, impulse of summer. The tang of coffee, the bright morning air, and I'm dreaming that the lost children walk again in the sun, as close as pain, unreachable as those in pain, as all-pervasive as waters rising over the crumbling shores of the eastern counties; fields under water after centuries, the contours of the land made strange. And yet some say that Time is like a small harbour on the Atlantic coast, a sea breeze tugging the sails. Let's go, and look for the living; longitude and magnitude, master mariners all.

And suddenly I'm ten years old, in a meadow with bees buzzing, and what am I holding in my hands—these flowers, these shadows—is it almost honey, is it snow? These memories seem to tap me on the shoulder, seem to be rather too forward for propriety. Downstairs, I can hear noises. As if the dishwasher had grown legs and was lumbering around the kitchen. I'd like to shake three pennies and drop them in a random fashion and let that be the answer to life's difficulties. I'm watching a man across the park. In and out of the streetlight-pools he goes, and I wonder if I'm that man. When we have acquired a child-like openness of mind, we shall certainly be helped to understand the secrets of the world. For a long time I used to go to bed early. Sometimes, when I had put out my candle, my eyes would close so quickly that I had not even time to say 'I'm going to sleep'. King Abdullah of Saudi Arabia is on a state visit to Britain. A British government minister said that Saudi Arabia and Britain have 'shared values'. Really. Democracy? Freedom of speech? Equality for women? Religious tolerance? Opposition to torture and capital punishment? Yet the two kingdoms (isn't ours a queendom?) have much in common insists … I wonder what happened to my Hofner semi-acoustic bass after I sold it for a hundred and twenty quid to that guitar shop in Newcastle. I guess I'll never know for sure.

8.

The invisible wind is redefining itself. It came out of nothing, but it's everywhere. Let's sit down at the table together and talk softly late into the night. In the place where the storyteller was the coming of night was marked as it was not in towns nor in modern homes. In repetition of traditions that were the people's own, like the table, the bench, the grandmother's chair, what was told was news of people they knew—the queen's daughter who herded geese, the king's son whose quest was for nothing less than the Water of Life. News of people we know and do not know. A massive blackout has left 86,000 homes without power in the Greater Manchester area. The Penan's way of life is under threat as commercial logging continues to destroy their home around them. A bent twig stuck in the trail may simply say 'we went this way', but complex arrangements of cut twigs, sticks and folded leaves can tell the Penan anything. Switch off the TV, let's talk late into the night. We talked, then stepped outside to see Orion and The Plough, the half-moon rising. When however, the pieces of the moon had united themselves together again in the world below, where darkness had always prevailed, it came to pass that the dead became restless and awoke from their sleep. I want to question the world more closely, and to feel the sun on my back, for perhaps I sleep, and dream, and walk on the paths of childhood.

Hello? Are you there? Who could be more of a stranger than a dead man? Almost the weekend, but I have to drive south on Sunday night and stay in the Holiday Inn at Egham. The writer is nobody. Fill in a self-assessment tax return. Install XSI on my laptop. Make doctor's appointment. Buy some ear-plugs. If only I had a better memory. An attention to life, sufficiently powerful and sufficiently separated from all practical interest, would thus include in an undivided present the entire past history of the conscious person. Hingis Quits Under Cocaine Cloud. The new wars of religion. Work life balance? Don't know where to turn? Call 0800 716017. 24-hour support, 365 days a year. The indivisible continuity of change is precisely what constitutes true duration. My grandmother lost her husband, aged thirty, to tuberculosis, leaving her with three small children. They often didn't have enough to eat. The two boys went off to war in 1939. He never talked to me about his war experiences. His life seems to have been lived so long ago. Under the cocaine cloud the climber coughs, till the cloud clears and views of fabled lowlands glimmer in the gloaming. The ice was crisp underfoot, the scree scurried and grass at last cushioned his boots. Soon he will reach the village where tribesmen will offer him honey and goats' milk, he will sleep on sheepskin and in the morning call 0800 716017. Hello? Are you there? Who could be more of a stranger than a dead man.

This morning I drove past a field with two horses in it, one white, one chestnut. They were running, and I slowed down to watch. They weren't an advert, they were real. The trees beyond them were autumn colours and the sky was clear apart from the tracks of a few aircraft. Horses running over grass under clear skies, with wind-blown autumn trees. It was as if my day had suddenly become a different day, or I had been taken outside of it by these creatures, which seemed so exotic at that moment of a long, boring drive. Why is it that as soon as I describe something to someone else, a note of falsehood enters? This morning he drove past a field in which two horses were running. It was striking for an instant, no more. It stirred something in him. Then he braked and checked his mirror and felt slightly irritated as another car overtook him. While driving past the field with the two horses he was preoccupied with the difficulty of finding his hotel, the third in three nights. Good evening sir, your room is ready. Please be advised that it is open to the sky, and that the walls are invisible, or should I say 'hard to see'. It will appear that you are out in the open, under the stars, in a field, and that in the morning you will wake to see two horses running, one white, one chestnut. Do not be alarmed. It's only a piece of make believe.

The Drill Hall Vaults is open. I hardly remember the deserted street and pale grey days in which it lived. The fathers are all gathered there, recalling incidents and lifting their tremendous moustaches. Every story tells the same one. Every accidental meeting is logged and archived. Every mouth speaks true. At roll call, I remember the waiting and the pale grey cry from the mouth of the Tyne, and yet I always thought you knew. Knew what? The cause of thunder. Why we age. Who walked with you on those amber evenings. Why he deserted. The waiting, and the slow trek though endless terraces where chimneys sang their smoky song and television aerials out-whistled the blackbirds, as if the clouds were us and we the mirror that reflected them, as if the skipping children were our thoughts. The cobblestones could be glazed with rain or a sahara of shifting sleep. In this house lived an old man. A strip of grass and a few stunted trees near the churchyard wall was an undiscovered Amazon. At night, foghorns sounded and welders' sparks twinkled across the river. Rhythm and blues blaring through the open window. Your brother's a hippy! From the top of the hill, the summer stretched across the city. Have you seen owt o' my bonny lad? 'Twas on the sea I spied him. His grave is green, but not wi' grass, and thou'll never lie beside him. Let's walk together on this amber evening. The Drill Hall Vaults is open and its pints are waiting.

She grabbed his scruff, shook his pockets loose, polished the world lens till it gleamed, then took him home to meet my life. It's 8.05am in the poem. A poem that may be read at 8.05 and may have been written at 8.05. Maybe. But the poem can make it any time it likes. They met and went back to her place and now it's been all of twenty years, real-time. Our research shows that most people staying in a hotel simply want a clean, comfortable place to get 'a good night's sleep'. To sleep through the good night. Or wander through its dark fields, its dreams, restless movements, painful memories, and the abiding sense of mystery that can overtake one in the complete darkness of a strange room in an unknown town. I sleep with the light on. I think positive thoughts: almond trees and evergreen oak above a carpet of flowers, terraced hillsides with cedars and a coastal path to the moorish watchtower, 'the view over the bay'. But the girls were tired, and the youngest needed to be carried. Bitten by insects, burned by the sun, and completely forgetting the world and all its cares. Heat, dust. Aircraft taking off and ceaseless traffic on the autoroute. The midday sun was unbearable, and there's still the complete darkness of a strange room to consider. Let's make it 8.05. It's 8:05am, 21st November. Frost on the garden, the neighbourhood quiet. Clear sky and a north-east wind. I sip tea (Assam). I don't long for anything.

Who will speak for the birds? They have no language of their own, flung here and there by windy air, and ignorant of charts. As if low-pressure systems grew on trees, which of course, they don't, at least not that I'm aware. Weather-vanes tell you nothing except perhaps that good people everywhere are not in vogue, despite plough-lines, skilful bricklaying and apprenticeships. Keep catalogues of laundry, you never know what's in the pockets, or whether old receipts and specious love-letters might redeem a wilting life. All around us there are the nebulous galaxies—eyes that are naked alone cannot see them. Give me my escallope shell of quiet, turn on the bathroom light I think there's a spider in here of immense proportions. I'm interrupting this semi-permanent hiatus to note that Baroque pearls are pearls with no definite shape. They are simply oddballs. The process model says 'if x=true then go to location B', and logic is a sort of compulsion. I'd like to see my brothers and sisters again, my schoolfriends, but they'd be grey with kindly eyes I wouldn't recognise. So the binary system kicks in, inviting 1 and 0 to be king. The drip of rainy leaves and that moist smell is 1, sleep and its confines 0, and although an algebraic law like this contains within itself the seeds of its demise, yet on this warm, rainy day in summer whose quality is forgetfulness and whose talent is for quiet and a sort of ease, it's what we take for truth.

14.

The kitchen is quiet at this late hour, but through the open door the sound of a TV — *Question Time*, the politicians and the people. Who is speaking for the birds? Sparrows seek asylum in the orderly sunlight, squabble for scraps in the disorderly breeze. She drove across the border. Her mother's tears. She's gone, gone, gone. The music drowns out the TV. The building workers from Poland are in that place, the cleaners from Latvia, maids from the Philippines, the marchers for Peace might be there. The gardens will be well-tended, and in the public parks football and games of hide-and-seek. Police say there were nearly 10,000 arrests during the dispute. On average, 3,000 extra officers were deployed each day. The miners were like gypsies, travelling miners you know, right round, they drifted, Lanchester, Annfield Plain, Marley Hill colliery and then when they all closed, they went to the coast pits. During the strike, the women had blossomed and started coming together and making decisions … but the men didn't want that; I mean most men. The fellow-feeling—I suppose I'd call it that—was like a form of Grace. A snowy morning, after the first shift had gone through the picket line, me and two others getting warm round a little bonfire. I was twenty-six. Things changed. Grace has both the meaning of self-adornment, as in the ego-self-image, and the true grace of simplicity and acceptance. The student of the *I Ching* eventually realises that the goal cannot be separated from the path.

When he was out of work he'd scrub the floor till it was spotless. He was a good man. When he gorra job he'd spend the money on drink. If he wasn't hyem by four o'clock, me mother would say, that's it, he's not coming hyem. We wouldn't see him, sometimes for days, till he'd spent aall his wages. The other women would send their bairns round with some coins. They'd say 'Me ma says to give this to Mrs. Bowman'. The adverts on Channel 5 go on a long time, and form a crass interlude to first-hand accounts of war veterans: *Forgotten Heroes: The Not Dead.* The future is Orange. Get there faster. The sixteenth hexagram: the enlightened man is watchful, therefore perceives the point in every situation where he is tempted to take hold. Precisely at this point he retreats and disengages. Then I turned back again in the teeth of the rain, and sat over the fire with the old man and woman talking of the sorrows of the people till late into the night. No two journeys to these islands are alike. The open boat plunged. Wind and spray. Between Paros and Mykenos, bright sunshine. That sense of freedom only comes with youth. Sure, it's an illusion, but it's a beautiful one and I wish I could get it back again, I really do. Doesn't everyone? That was just before we met. To hell with freedom. Lassie lie near me. Long have we parted been. Les choses les plus simple, jamais oublié.

The things you see at 4am! Do people still have their milk delivered in glass bottles? Without my glasses the streetlights float like faery lights across the park. St. Elmo's Fire. The bushes thrash about in the wind. First person singular present tense. What else is there? I think about my father thirty years dead. John and I are not on speaking terms. I stress about work and what I have to do tomorrow. How will my children live? That's future tense. The will-o'-the-wisp lights in the short-sighted dark. The long-sighted page. Is it all happening in a continuous present? he asks / asked / will ask. What time is it? All clocks moving through the ether are slowed down compared to clocks at rest in the ether. One would have to distinguish between 'apparent' and 'true' space and time measurements, with the further proviso that 'true' dimensions and 'true' times could never be determined by any experimental procedure. That clock on my wall, its numbers are blurred. Long have we parted been, lassie my dearie. I remember talking to an old man when I was a child. He was my cousin's grandad. He said that as a young man he came to Newcastle from Yorkshire to look for work. That was in 1900. In the narrow streets near the river he was surprised to see women sitting outside their front doors, smoking clay pipes, as he'd never seen such a thing in Yorkshire. Why should I think about this at four o'clock in the morning?

A river runs nearby, small, dark and fast-moving, carrying dead leaves and making a gurgling noise that mingles with car horns, sirens and revved-up engines. The river has white foam floating on it; it's a line of drainage from the South Downs to the North Sea. It's a line of thought through curve and parabola to the point of calm, reflecting, under streetlights, house-fronts already undermined. Under flood, green-lanes and beauty-spots become the menace they maybe always were. It's a recurring fear, it comes in dreams, when the moonlit meadow clings, ankle-deep, rushes and asphodel shift underfoot, and the land is unreliable, prone to flood, seasonally, and will-o'-the-wisp. Prone to lonely progress through the past and future tense, to a subjunctive tide and surge and dark water reflecting the pier and harbour lights. At least in dreams, asphodel and clinging mud. At least in thoughts of lonely progress. Now I'm in a small motel in Staines, Surrey. Outside my window I can see McDonald's, Waitrose, Tesco Home and Computerworld. He who would valiant be, gainst all disaster. So sung the schoolchildren in the wooden hall. The wave hit me and the world was blurred and silent. In 1953 storm surge in the North Sea combined with exceptional tides. Crumbling shores in the eastern counties, fields under water after centuries, the tides persistent as a line of enquiry following a wave's progress through loneliness to breaking point. Lovers' walks, green-lanes, beauty-spots, become menace they maybe always were, clinging, ankle-deep, rushes and asphodel shifting underfoot.

All this talk of asphodel is getting on my nerves. Gimme a break! I'm not ready to go into the netherworld just yet, not even limbo or the Elysian fields. Et In Arcadia Ego. I'd hate to be the one to spoil things. The Blue Meanie in the psychedelic world of rainbows and flowers. But young Lycidas is dead and daffadillies fill their cups with tears. The Summer of Love. Daffodils scattered on seats in the concert hall, light shows during the gig. It was all so innocent in those days. But, of course, there is no 'present moment'. Events that appear simultaneous to one observer would appear to have taken place at different times to observers in different states of motion. Thus, it is necessary to speak of relativity of simultaneity. My mother's eldest brother died of pneumonia at the age of twenty. The family didn't possess a photograph of him. This young man, still a boy really, passed into memory. Seventy years later, my mother was at an exercise class for the elderly, when a woman she barely knew came up to her. 'Are you Mary Bowman? This is yours'. A photograph of her brother, taken in a seaside photo booth, kept by this woman as a memento of her childhood sweetheart. I don't know how my mother felt, seeing that face again after all those years. Is it all happening in a continuous present? In the personal recollections of innumerable people, a continuing song, the lay of the great journey, collective and incomplete.

The belief that a person's life in time on Earth is repetitive may have been an inference from the observed repetitiveness of phenomena in the environment. It's only quarter to eleven, but tomorrow is already banging at the door. Don't let it in! It'll be here again soon enough, when I have my Breakfast-To-Go (available from reception 24 hours a day) then peer round nervously trying to find the exit. Try the back door, it opens onto green fields. Here at the front we have to contend with the sleeping world on its silent journey through space and the car headlights circling and circling. As if we were somehow culpable, we have to contend with the Halloween witches who smile and offer us children, the door-to-door salesmen who try to buy us, the postmen who take away the letters we'd been longing to receive. Try the side door, you'll see Morris dancers jangling bells the size of drumlins. Here at the front the open-cast mining company has come to dig our garden, our ten-year old son insists we call him 'sir', police officers arrive to turn themselves in, the window cleaner smears dirt on the windows and aimless delivery men offer us directions. They say, try the back door, it's much safer that way. Indeed, I am sure it is, but in the meantime I have ample opportunity to ponder on the irreversibility and inexorability of the passage of time. Unlike other living creatures, they know that their lives may be cut short at any moment.

20.

Outside, it's well below freezing but the coffee in here tastes good. SMS: Hi, hope u r feeling OK. Looking forward to seeing u 2morrow. Love Dadx. Everyone I know leads a life that has no time in it. Not literally, of course, that would be impossible. But a three hour journey down the motorway, a meeting, catch up on some emails, then head to the hotel and prepare a presentation for tomorrow? The Christmas trees in the car park and faery lights on the bushes have voices like female TV presenters; low and musical, authoritative, but ultimately insincere. I know it all. I'm learning to leave my history at the door and to think uncontrollably at the most inconvenient times of the world my enemy, my friend, my teacher. It's a state of mind, home. From my hotel window I watch a car with dark windows take the corner very fast, almost losing control, then screech off into the night. The position and the velocity of an object cannot both be measured exactly, at the same time, even in theory. The very concepts of exact position and exact velocity together, in fact, have no meaning in nature. Ordinary experience provides no clue of this principle. My enemy, my friend, my teacher. It's her I'm thinking of. Without her I'd be nothing. A speck in the infinite. Of course, the behaviour of matter and radiation on the atomic scale often seems peculiar, and the consequences of quantum theory are accordingly difficult to understand and to believe.

The twenty-second hexagram: doubt and fear cause us to split from our path. We are afraid to let matters take their own course. We think we have to influence the situation through some plan. They want my iris, my fingerprints and my DNA. They want my skin colour and the location of my memories. They want my shoe size and my next of kin. They want my fears, my hopes, my blood type and my National Insurance Number. I want the wind to shake the trees. They want me on record and I have no plan. Here's a plan: pack my hairdryer/adapter/mobile phone charger. Take to the open road. A free-born man of the travelling people. But how will my children live? QUESTION: The main pillar of the house, what does it preach? ANSWER: The Zen master wakes up early in the morning and takes care of his pupils. In an ordinary house, the father, from early morning, raises his voice and looks after his family's affairs. A snowy morning, after the first shift had gone through the picket line, me and two others getting warm round a little bonfire. I was twenty-six. Things changed. When he was out of work he'd scrub the floor till it was spotless. That's a memory of her memory. I want the road outside my door, which leads nowhere, to lead, as it used to, to a future filled with medieval archers, the adventures of Dan Dare, the Durham Miners' Gala and exotic lands from a child's atlas.

Integrate. Assemble. Optimize. Please read your *Participant's Guide*. Launch the integration management console to configure host services. Suchlike phrases and the wound in the wallows bears bruntly the burden. Close up the book of days, it's the night that steals the show. The larks are gone from the fields, enter the children, in flocks, to stand with us, as it were, bemused, to watch light play on the levels and shallows. What air will glide upon each moment? The wind from the Atlantic makes us stand close together for warmth. It's like living on the Moon, says John, or on a space station. Please read your *Participant's Guide*: shake three pennies and drop them in a random fashion. Add the three coins up and write the resulting number on a piece of paper. Fourth Line: she is the treasure of the house. It's a state of mind, home. Cold kitchen floor, rain on the glass, the sleeping houses' watchful windows. The hum of dreams across the city gave way to something remembered at daybreak, when the swifts across the park rehearsed the names of drifting friends. Wing-flick and slow beat, migrations and sedentary populations spread across the surface of the globe. She is the treasure of the house. She seems a long way away tonight; a phone call is no substitute. My enemy, my friend, my teacher. Live with compassion. Work with compassion. Die with compassion. Meditate with compassion. Enjoy with compassion. When problems come, experience them with compassion. Integrate, assemble, optimize. Bear bruntly the burden.

Get the exclusive adventure pack Citröen 4x4. Everyone's got an opinion, what's yours worth? Comet: we live electricals. Someone's knocking on my room door. My best manly voice convinces them they've got the wrong room. A feast of ideas from Waitrose. The debugger isn't working on this software. Now it is, thank god. On the iPod, 'Dirt Road Blues'. Now a folk song: 'Cruel' … were my parents, that took my love from me, cruel were the press gang who took him off to sea. I read somewhere that it was hard to sink sailing ships with cannons, so the aim was to kill as many sailors as possible with small shot, chained-together cannon balls and so on, before boarding the ship. I read it during the celebrations over Trafalgar. At that battle, a captured Spanish sailor was still wearing the clown's outfit he had on when he was press-ganged coming out of the theatre. This is what I'm thinking, now typing. Then suddenly, we are no longer in touch with these experiences. A memory, a fantasy, a fear has snatched us away into the dim, seductive twilight of unawareness. Dead men can't talk, but if they could, you wouldn't be able to shut them up. But who could be more of a stranger than a dead man? The debugger is working now, thank goodness, and the knocking on my door has stopped. It's midnight. I should get some sleep. I guess this could be considered serial music. I guess it could be considered a mosaic.

An accurate dageurreotyped portrait of a commonplace face; a carefully fenced, highly cultivated garden, with neat borders and delicate flowers; but no glance of a bright, vivid physiognomy, no open country, no fresh air, no blue hill, no bonny neck. Walled courtyards enclose fine gardens, orchards and a herb garden, and the surrounding country park contains rare breeds of sheep and cattle. On 9th July 1800, Joseph Carpenter was indicted for feloniously stealing, on the 7th of June, two muslin neck-handkerchiefs, the property of Charlotte Hartley, spinster. They were two muslin handkerchiefs; I then opened them, and told him they were the property of Miss Hartley; he turned round, was very much frightened, and begged I would not say any thing. GUILTY (Aged 29.) of stealing the handkerchiefs. Transported for seven years. The decoration includes superb woodcarving by Grinling Gibbons, plasterwork and painted murals and ceilings by Louis Lageurre, and there is a fine collection of portraits. The Great Staircase is the most elaborate of its kind in an English house. Several rooms featured in the BBC's *Pride and Prejudice* and *Jane Eyre*. Elizabeth Wilson was indicted for feloniously stealing, on the 1st of October, six window curtains, value 12s, two head draperies value 7s, 10 tassels, value 7s and vallances, value 3s. Prisoner's defence. I had a drop of liquor too much; I did not know what I was doing. Q. Did she appear to be in liquor?—A. Yes; she did appear to be in liquor. GUILTY, Death, aged 33. 30th Oct 1805.

You'd all the front steps to scrub, and the stairs, and there were miles of them, carpeted of course, and you'd be brushing those with a hand brush and dustpan, no Hoover or anything. Those had to be done by seven o'clock. If the mistress was entertaining, there was dinner to serve in the evening. It was at eight o'clock, with about eight courses, and you didn't get finished until after ten. Time off amounted to one half day a week. It is a form of the unconscious (that part of the mind containing memories and impulses of which the individual is not aware) common to mankind as a whole and originating in the inherited structure of the brain ... the like of which we have never experienced before and probably will never experience again ... we had found something special in the joint struggle ... all classes, beliefs and political view points worked together for a common goal. (Doreen, written account of her activism, 2003). The serial yob, who has terrorised her neighbours on Newcastle's Newbiggin Hall estate for years, tried to tell officers that she had been fitting a carpet for a friend and forgot to take the knife out her pocket. But the 18-year-old pleaded guilty to carrying a bladed article in public before Newcastle Magistrates. It is distinct from the personal unconscious, which arises from the experience of the individual, and according to Jung, it contains archetypes, or universal primordial images and ideas. In reality the pattern of women's trajectories of activism is one of continuity.

One winter's evening, with Christmas a few weeks away and the family due home from a shopping trip to town, bearing exotic clothes and consumer items, while outside there's cold wind and sleet, document types could be obtained from the on-line server. The diagram shows how to set the document-type associated with a recieve node. I before E except after C. Receive node. I must clear my mind so I can enjoy the evening with my family. Everyone acknowledges that money is an important factor. The central question here is whether the Americans are sacrificing short-term security gains for long-term instability in Iraq (Rear Admiral James Smith, Radio 4). Tomorrow's going to be another working day, and I'm just trying … Hello Helen, yes, I'll tell her you called. What are you doing for Christmas? She wanted to know what presents she should buy for the girls. Helen's father was sent to a Siberian Gulag. He managed to escape and travel back to Poland by horseback, and after the war he made a new life in England. Looking back makes you aware that you're part of a continuum. What will our descendents say about us? How will my children live? It's all in the hands of Fate, there's nothing that I can do. Change, return, success. All movement is accomplished in six stages, and the seventh brings return. The seven is the number of the young light. It forms when darkness is increased by one. They'll be home soon. I'll get the tea on. Action brings good fortune.

Not wanting to live is identical with not wanting to die. Waxing and waning make one curve. I sat for hours under a one hundred year-old pear tree practicing the *I Ching* technique. All sorts of undeniably remarkable results emerged. Later that night the kitchen was quiet, but through the open door the sound of a TV — *The Secret Millionaire*. Voice-over. But who will speak for the birds and the wildlife of our shrinking island? At night I see foxes slink, hungry, by day birds squabble over scraps of bread. The unregulated free market, that's what keeps me on my toes. Life's Good—get all the smiles you want. The future is Orange. Get there faster. Career there at an unstoppable speed. Tomorrow I'll be back on the road. Tonight, the moon hangs big and yellow over the house tops. The lunatic season. Children dressed as ghosts. The living dead knock on my door and ask for sweets. It's disturbing. They're daubed in fake blood. I want friends around, not strangers, and who could be more of a stranger than a dead man? And listen to this, a letter to me from Her Majesty's Revenue and Customs: … a copy of some HMRC data about families, including yours, has been lost. This data includes your and your children's names and dates of birth … The police are now conducting a search. How can we know who we are when our data is lost? We're in limbo, under the yellow moon. Waxing and waning in one curve.

Number twenty-nine. The colour of the young light. Show me the colour of your money, that's more important. Precisely at this point he retreats and disengages. Really, it's as if a door had been closed, a door of perception, and my fingers were in the hinge. Sticky fingers, that's what he had, he got made treasurer of the union branch, and then one day he disappeared with the money. Drank it all. He wouldn't come home after that, slept rough. He was ashamed. It's about the beer. Carling's great British appeal owes a lot to its exceptionally well-balanced flavour and aroma. We know that Carling drinkers love the balance of thirst-quenching refreshment with a trademark bite ... Beer is one of the world's oldest beverages, possibly dating back to the 6th millennium BCE, and is recorded in the written history of ancient Egypt and Mesopotamia. And even, though all around us creep intimations of immortal soap-stars, lonesome hobos, delirious lottery winners, economic false dawns and early nights, yet we live in a darkened country where money doesn't grow on trees and doing your best with your foot forward on that shifting path might take you by surprise. A trademark bite. Those dogs frolicking across the park, do they have a 'trademark bite'? No, they just have a bite, isn't that enough? But look, the lights are on at the ironworks. The rubber factory is bouncing back. Production is at an all-time high, but the workers complain of being over-stretched. The economic miracle can't work its wonders forever.

In view of its occurrence among organically healthy individuals, déjà vu commonly has been regarded as psychogenic and as having its origin in some partly forgotten memory, fantasy, or dream. It was late. The office was quiet, only the hum of my computer, the noise from the aircon. The chairs were at odd angles to desks, as if they had invisible occupants. I didn't like the feeling of being alone there, and was about to leave, when my phone rang. You're on floor five aren't you, the caller said. I'm on my way up … They didn't give their name. A hoax. Forget it. It's time to leave anyway. It's just I have this strange feeling that I've been through this before, and I know who this caller is. I'm still not ready for them, so I'd better leave now. Walking through the city I reflected on what a strange thing memory is. Déjà vu: memory, fantasy or dream. Virtual memory is a scheme that gives users the illusion of working with a large block of contiguous memory space (perhaps even larger than real memory). O sleep it is a gentle thing. Switch off the TV. Check the kitchen appliances are off, lock the front door. Lights out. Well, maybe leave the bedside lamp on for a while. I didn't like the feeling of being alone there, and was about to leave, when my phone rang. You're on floor five aren't you, the caller said. I'm on my way up … While I waited, I consulted the *I Ching*.

The leaves that are being blown across the grass look like small, scuttling creatures. Sun and rain together. Autumn wind blowing leaves across the park. Autumn after autumn comes and goes and the dead leaves retain their spring form imprinted like a memory but transformed into dryness and decay. The sun is in Capricorn and the constellations turn through the branches at night. The Celts believed that the dead were closer to the world of the living during the period of long nights leading up to the solstice, that the deceased would come back to life and cause havoc such as sickness or damaged crops. Autumn after autumn, milder now than when I was young. The world's weather is changing, the Holocene period, is it coming to an end? Another name for the Holocene that is sometimes used is the Anthropogene, the 'Age of Man', as it witnessed all of humanity's recorded history and the rise and fall of its civilizations. The world's whole history is imprinted on its form—drumlins in the valleys, the shadow of extinct volcanoes in the soft English uplands. Firefox is installing your updates and will restart soon. Google 'glaciation terms': Ablation, abrasion, accumulation. Drift: an archaic term for heterogeneous sediment (presumed to be deposited by drifting icebergs, perhaps in Noah's flood!). Includes and retained in stratified drift, but not in till. (Till: Deposits of a glacier). One day, in the Holocene interglacial, leaves were blown across the park. A couple walked hand-in-hand in winter sunshine. Light rain on the uplands.

Hexagram thirty-two. Duration. The images of thunder and wind, as elements which always accompany each other, symbolize relationships which endure. Thus we are counselled by this hexagram to be steady. We are told that pressure is part and parcel of all work and helps to keep us motivated. But excessive pressure can lead to stress, which undermines performance, is costly to employers and can make people ill. Tomorrow I'll throw a sickie. It keeps us motivated. It's part and parcel of the cycle of samsara. On Friday, I did. I've been thinking about it all weekend. Restlessness as an enduring condition brings misfortune. I sometimes wish I had an insight into the true meaning of Reality, or perhaps a private undisclosed income which rendered me a gentleman of leisure. US stocks closed mostly higher on Friday, for a fourth consecutive session, as hopes for further interest rate cuts and a nascent plan to help sub-prime borrowers lifted a range of financial companies and homebuilders. A Thawing Market: rising temperatures are slowly revealing the Arctic's resources, making it the new frontier for an influx of businesses, workers and residents. I know I can rely on my friends. Lalani is expected to force through cost cutting which will lead to job losses among BT Global Services' worldwide workforce of 37,000. Pressure is part and parcel of work. No-one is ever to blame. Anonymous donors to party funds, money transferred via proxies. This, in my weakness, I think about much, Hexagram thirty-two. Restlessness as an enduring condition brings misfortune.

Here i am again, in Melbourne this time, been back since Oct 13th so it's a month+ ... How's tricks? i read that yr website was 'down'? or maybe yr email so perhaps you wont be reading this for a while?! So Helen's in college??? Where??? Studying what??? And soon off to Germany??? My my my how the time doth go ... Time molds us. Without past there is no present, and the I cannot be imagined. We use words, when we can't be together, words in cyberspace, in the ether. SMS: Hi, hope u r feeling OK. Looking forward to seeing u 2morrow. Love Dadx. Language is the new Spiritus Mundi! You'll have to forgive my silence. Work has turned nasty, and I'm preoccupied and busy a lot of the time (moan, moan in true British fashion). I can hardly remember my own name these days. I'll try and remember to email you with a full report, or at least put it on my blog. School photographs of my children and the words of a song I heard in strange circumstances once are merging with the sound of rain on the window and the night, the long night of winter, that stretches a moment like a violin string, out of tune and snapping, that makes the paths dark and hard to follow. I can barely remember my own name these days. Fertile forgetfulness. It pushes us to sound soul and spirit in the name of spirit and soul. It helps us clear the various paths of consciousness.

When it's time to get up for work, the sky is still full of stars, the streetlights are shining. The world has tilted on its axis to face the universe. So much empty space. It's like the hour when an invalid, who has been obliged to start on a journey and to sleep in a strange hotel, awakens in a moment of illness and sees with glad relief a streak of daylight shewing under his bedroom door. Who am I? The ultimate question. I wish I knew the answer. I am the neighbour who drives a green Nissan. I am ... Who is the person asking who I am? I don't know. My personal data has been lost, or is at least unreliable. My new manager is making my life difficult and it's keeping me awake at night. It's not personal, he only knows one of my selves. The rain makes me wet, but it's not personal, it just happens. If only I could sleep at night. When a man is asleep, he has in a circle round him the chain of the hours. Is dying like sleeping, but without dreams? People sleep more in midwinter, there's less light. Who could be more of a stranger than a sleeping man? Who is he? Is he like my neighbour who has an expensive telescope and invites me over in the evenings to look at Sirius or Aldebaran or the moons of Jupiter? Is he contemplating things so immensely distant, the sleeping man? Is that why he's so strange?

34.

You'll have to forgive my silence. I can hear the rain, but I can't see it. It's windy and I can hear drips from the window ledges and heavy downpour on the pavement. Is it morning? There's not much distinction between night and day. The days are like candles in a gloomy room (that sounds good). Not much distinction between sleep and waking. Those Halloween tricksters are gone now, but I keep thinking I can hear them. The winters aren't crisp and cold anymore, no white sunshine, icicles and snowdrifts. One morning I sat up in bed and scraped the frost from the bedroom window to see whose face looking in at me? Or was that a dream? Once, the wide, white world was whirling under the wheeling weather. All the 'W's sang together. Now it's only R, the dreary rain running in rills round the road. Climatologists know what the rest of us only surmise. Mais où sont les neiges d'antan? I can't help feeling some nostalgia for them. Snow and hail and slush and sleet. In fact, frozen precipitation has been classified into seven forms of snow crystals and three types of particles— graupel (granular snow pellets, also called soft hail), sleet (partly frozen ice pellets), and hail (hard spheres of ice). I remember crunching through deep snow, holding my mother's hand. When snow melts in the spring, the resulting runoff feeds rivers and supplies water for irrigation and other human enterprises. The dreary rain runs in rills. The reservoirs are full to bursting.

You'll have to forgive my silence. I should write more. Yesterday we went to a Christmas fête at our local school, and a poet had a stall there, a bookfull of samples and a price list. I asked him for a poem about snow, and he wrote it in invisible ink. Is that an icicle or his frozen finger? Snow, blanketing the world in silent white/ muffling sound and making bright the night … He didn't say that at temperatures above about -40° C, ice crystals form around minute particles of dust or chemical substances that float in the air, but that, at lower temperatures, crystals form directly from water vapour. But why should that concern him? Prices start from £25. When we left the fête it was raining and quite windy. Although precipitation has increased in the northern hemisphere, the air is too thick and dark for wiccan magick, too wavy and ecstatic for the silent process known as snowmaking to descend to our realm. When I got home I took out the poet's card. It was invisible. Poems for weddings, new job, greetings cards, the birth of a baby. Traditional or free forms. There were no schemes for the exotic transformations within the dream-work which established in retrospect a real-time disposition for traumatic amnesia. Back home we looked at adverts for a floor-cleaning robot. Jane called. It turned colder during the afternoon, crisp by nightfall. It started snowing. The flakes drifted from the dark. Exotic transformations within the dream-work. Muffling sound and making bright the night.

Police roadblocks slowed down the traffic going into Nottinghamshire. Resistance to the strike hardened there, and it was the focus of flying pickets from all over the country. And yet, it was a time of such freedom, hitch-hiking down motorways in the cabs of 40-ton trucks or the saloon cars of besuited executives. Meanwhile, at the summer solstice, strange herbs were smoked and stars glittered in the sparks from the campfire. Later, it rained, but the songs continued: Ettrick forest is a fair forest/ in it grows many a seemly tree. What we have lost over the past four centuries is not the spirit of song or the flash of minstrel invention, but a sense of a community to whose members these ballads were both fact and romance, history and entertainment. The rumble in the coalfields continued. It was a defining moment in British industrial relations, and significantly weakened the British trades union movement. The use of power in the *I Ching* refers mostly to what we say and think. External force is always incorrect. And yet, we can't help thinking, or wishfully thinking even … Craving can vanish in awakening to the absurdity of the assumptions which underlie it. There were schemes for the exotic transformations within the dream-work. Meanwhile, snow fell on the uplands, and groups of striking miners huddled round fires. It fell upon the Lammas tide, when husbands win their hay … the like of which we have never experienced before and probably will never experience again … Not in the realms of thick, dark air.

The texture and density of fallen snow undergo constant change. As for ice: if a shear stress or force is applied to a sample of ice for a long time, the sample will first deform elastically and will then continue to deform plastically, with a permanent alteration of shape. The strike began to fall apart in the early months of 1985, with miners in many regions reluctantly returning to work. The winter had been particularly harsh that year and most families were unable to afford heating as the NUM's funds had been seized by the government in October of '84. A shear stress might make exotic transformations within the dream-work. The hiss of a gas fire, a slight ringing in my ears; this is what passes for silence. Thoughts about tomorrow quieted by writing them in a notebook (this one); this is what passes for calm. Who am I? I am the person who remembers. Remembers what? What is written in the book of days and nights. In the firelight, in a little two-up two-down in the west end of Newcastle, snow piled up on the pavements. A note sent up the chimney's draught to the household deity. A shear stress. Exotic transformations within the dream-work. The strike was called off after it had failed to interrupt power supplies during the National Grid's highest ever demand, during the cold winter of that year. The subtle thief of youth. A shear stress or force applied to a sample of ice. Forms change and deform, elastically then plastically.

The poet left me his calling card. He lived where sailors from the docks wind up their umbrellas and swap tales with the matron. I had some questions to put to him. Are owls as intelligent as they say? Do bats know the meaning of colour? Why is there a black cat in here? His answers took many forms: complex theory-driven word-play, rhymes about getting older and visiting his mother in a care home, a minstrel lay, an advertising jingle, the hiss of the wind over endless plains, the silence of the stars. With his out-of-tune piano in the smoky bar, he had an answer for everything, even for death. His theories seemed nothing but mist and rumour, like a cloud of bees. I told him I should have consulted the *I Ching*; how in practice, one 'creates' a hexagram by casting lots in one of several ways. The hexagram is built up from the bottom, line by line, by successive lots. Solid lines have the number nine, broken lines have the number six. Listen poet, [wu wei] … is an action so well in accordance with things that its author leaves no trace of himself in his work. Solid lines represent yang (the male cosmic principle), while broken lines represent yin (the female cosmic principle). These two principles explain all being and all change by their ceaseless interaction. Each hexagram is made up from two trigrams, which the legendary emperor Fu Hsi (24th century BC) is said to have discovered on the back of a tortoise.

There is Lucy, emerging from her dream of selfhood into the world, which is big and wide and adolescent. The Future is Orange. If you have even the slightest interest in technology, you'll be well aware that Apple is launching its iPhone in the UK tomorrow. The child is walking to school. The sun is shining. The field is white with frost. The sun is coming up over the leafless trees and the child's breath is like a familiar spirit. A patient with Wernicke's aphasia has difficulty understanding language; his own speech is typically fluent but is empty of content and characterized by circumlocutions, a high incidence of vague words like 'thing', and sometimes neologisms and senseless 'word salad'. Gaffe-prone George W. Bush has been surprisingly defeated in the race for the 2007 Foot In Mouth award. But which hapless Brit beat him to the dreaded prize? Sainsbury's Life Insurance, 'for protecting your den and your cubs'. 500 Nectar points. The child is walking to school. The sun is shining, the field is white with frost, the sun is coming up over the leafless trees. The child's breath is like a familiar spirit. The world can seem holy sometimes. The morning star is in the southern sky, a mist is rising over the frosted fields. Venus shines in the sky like a familiar spirit. 'Holy' may have meant no more than 'lucky', and 'ghost' no more than 'mammal' or breathing entity … we cannot attribute to such words a Christian sense in a pre-Christian context. Lucky breathing entity.

40.

I used to believe in myself, but now I'm agnostic. If the face fits, wear it. Who's that knocking on the door? Look at them, Halloween trick-or-treaters—pointed hats and black cloaks. Such were the human witches, the fifth column of Satan on earth, his front-line agents in the struggle for control of the spiritual world. There's no need to worry, no need to stress. Around the world Lexmark helps 75% of the world's bankers and retailers, and now they can help you at home! That's OK then, I'll settle down and watch this programme on Channel 4 — *This is Civilization* tells the story of modern art and culture, from its beginnings in artists like Picasso, Klee and Mondrian, right up to the present day. But what about the *Malleus Maleficarum?* The Hammer of the Witches? They had been persecuting and burning witches locally. From now on, a general mandate was given, or implied. A few jelly beans should do it, then switch the lights out and pretend we're not in. And indeed, it was in the wake of the greatest of all purges—perhaps in revulsion against it—that the solidity of the witch-hunters began to give way. Lexmark printers do appear to be reliable and have good print quality. Outside, in the dark street, pumpkin lanterns are burning low, and the last tricksters have drifted back to their homes to take off their grotesque make-up ready for school tomorrow. Their faces will fit once again. They can believe in themselves.

[It] was considered the end of the summer period, the date on which the herds were returned from pasture. It was also a time when the souls of those who had died were believed to return to visit their homes. It's a strange feeling when one of your own children reminds you of a brother or sister you've fallen out with and haven't seen for many years. That's a sort of karma I guess. It's a way of learning to be a better person, isn't it? People set bonfires on hilltops for relighting their hearth fires for the winter and to frighten away evil spirits, and they sometimes wore masks and other disguises to avoid being recognized by the ghosts thought to be present. The period was also favourable for divination on matters such as marriage, health, and death. This latter is an interesting phenomenon: the total cessation of life processes that eventually occurs in all living organisms, its precise definition remains controversial. But what about Life? Despite the enormous fund of information that each of the biological specialities has provided us with, it is a remarkable fact that there is no generally accepted definition of life. Are life and death the same? Man tends to define in terms of the familiar. But the fundamental truths may not be familiar. My child reminds me of my brother who lives (?) I don't know where. We don't know what life is, we don't know what death is. Something connects us to those we may never see again.

42.

Coke Adds Life! Thirst-quenching, effervescing, lip-smacking, excreting, breathing, moving, eating. That's life! But many such properties are either present in machines that nobody is willing to call alive, or absent from organisms that everybody is willing to call alive. A visitor from another planet, judging from the enormous numbers of automobiles on the Earth and the way in which cities and landscapes have been designed for the special benefit of motorcars, might well believe that automobiles are not only alive but are the dominant life form on the planet. Excreting, breathing, moving, eating. That's life! And remembering? Brimming with radical intent, [he] presents a startling vision of the countryside in decline, marginalised and repackaged for the tourist industry. There are the voices of those mid-seventeenth century political and religious radicals who considered the poorest beggars, even 'rogues, thieves, whores, and cut purses' as 'every whit as good' as the great ones of the earth. The books and pamphlets published by the Ranters have in their titles a MacSweeney ring: *A Single Eye all Light, no Darkness, The Smoke of the Bottomlesse Pit, Copps Return to the wayes of Truth, Strange Newes from Newgate and the Old-Baily*. The road cuts through the South Downs, and the cars, seemingly endless all the long summer's day, drown out the skylarks and meadow pipits. Drovers' tracks, footpaths, ley lines. The possibility of walking away from the world of 'coercion, violence, property, triviality'. Walking was seen as an aid to the recovery of memory, creative expression and connecting to the divine.

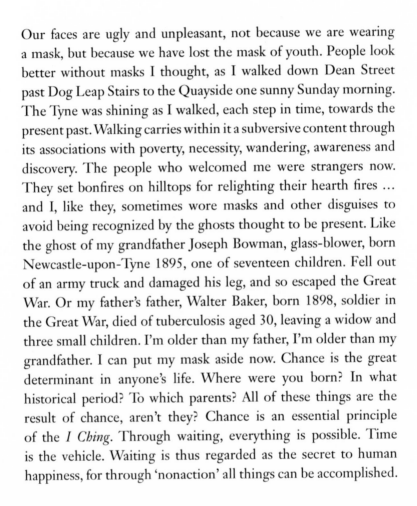

Our faces are ugly and unpleasant, not because we are wearing a mask, but because we have lost the mask of youth. People look better without masks I thought, as I walked down Dean Street past Dog Leap Stairs to the Quayside one sunny Sunday morning. The Tyne was shining as I walked, each step in time, towards the present past. Walking carries within it a subversive content through its associations with poverty, necessity, wandering, awareness and discovery. The people who welcomed me were strangers now. They set bonfires on hilltops for relighting their hearth fires ... and I, like they, sometimes wore masks and other disguises to avoid being recognized by the ghosts thought to be present. Like the ghost of my grandfather Joseph Bowman, glass-blower, born Newcastle-upon-Tyne 1895, one of seventeen children. Fell out of an army truck and damaged his leg, and so escaped the Great War. Or my father's father, Walter Baker, born 1898, soldier in the Great War, died of tuberculosis aged 30, leaving a widow and three small children. I'm older than my father, I'm older than my grandfather. I can put my mask aside now. Chance is the great determinant in anyone's life. Where were you born? In what historical period? To which parents? All of these things are the result of chance, aren't they? Chance is an essential principle of the *I Ching*. Through waiting, everything is possible. Time is the vehicle. Waiting is thus regarded as the secret to human happiness, for through 'nonaction' all things can be accomplished.

The big screen in the corner of the room has me mesmerised. It offers up a version of the world. All bugs fixed in the next version. Right now, as I write, there's a documentary about bar-girls in Bangkok whose aim in life is to find a foreign husband. Villages in rural Thailand have 'Best Foreign Husband' festivals, beautiful young women fêting portly and balding conquests from Birmingham and Frankfurt. Next a documentary about Antarctica. Once, long before I knew about CO_2 levels and the threat to the West Antarctic ice-sheet, I was queuing for a train ticket in Liverpool Street station, London, to get me to Brentwood, Essex, where I'd been offered a job. I had to get there by 5pm, and I'd hitch-hiked with empty pockets from the Midlands. I reached the kiosk to find I had no money. Must have lost my last fiver somewhere, and was faced with being stranded in what was, to me, an unknown city. I stood aside to let the next person through, a smart-suited Japanese businessman. He turned to me: 'How much do you need'? He peeled off a note from a roll and handed it to me. That gesture of charity has magnified in my mind during the intervening years. But putting it down here diminishes it somehow. Too late though. I've given you a version of it. There are now at least three versions: in my mind, in your mind, on the page. There is no one reality. Each of us inhabits a separate universe.

There is no one reality. Each of us inhabits a separate universe. That's not speaking metaphorically. This is the hypothesis of reality suggested by recent developments in quantum physics. Reality in a dynamic universe is non-objective. Consciousness is the only reality. So reality means the memories of each person? That dog that I'm watching scampering across the park in the chill autumn fog, running until he's out of sight in the gloom. Is he in a separate universe? We can confirm that your order was sent from our Fulfilment Centre. Tomorrow is the shortest day, St. Lucy's day, the winter solstice. Four more shopping days till Christmas, and the Sony Wii is out of stock everywhere. The Wii handset is a piece of advanced technology; it uses an accelerometer and a gyrometer to measure motion and tilt, and likewise utilizes both infrared and Bluetooth technology to interact with a sensor bar and to send information to the Wii console. The universe begins to look more like a great thought than like a great machine. M-Theory is defined in eleven dimensional space-time with ten dimensions of space and one dimension of time. F-Theory may contain two dimensions of time and ten dimensions of space. We believe that a multiverse of universes exist like bubbles floating in Nothing. Like a star at dawn, lightning in a summer cloud, a phantom and a dream. Mind no longer appears as an accidental intruder … we ought rather to hail it as the creator and governor of the realm of matter.

As we drove towards the bridge over the Wear at Sunderland, we caught sight of the Saxon church between the university building and the Comet superstore. In the winter sunshine it looked incongruous, like something placed there by a time machine. After an hour of driving south it was dark. The A1 was busy, and we sang Christmas carols to pass the time, revelling in the sense of nostalgia that these songs evoke. Look, if you want me to take on that project you have to be prepared to give me the technical support I need. 'Management by decree' won't get you anywhere. I don't want to be old. My brother can be infuriating at times, but at least he's older than me. My mother was better this time. Back to the A1, the noise of the engine, no talking. 'Twas night, calm night, the moon was high. To the left, the fields were in mist which was lit up by the moon, a sight so beautiful I almost swerved the car looking at it. Trees, black and skeletal, and pools of standing water like eyes looking at us from another time. 'Twas night, calm night, the moon was high. The dead men stood together. He wrote also of nature. He knew that the earth was a sphere. He had a sense of latitude and the annual movement of the sun into the north and south hemispheres from the evidence of varying lengths of shadows. He knew that the moon influenced the cycle of the tides.

What a dream I had! Up a narrow flight of stairs, in a narrow little room, a window wide enough to view the world. Family visits, with plentiful children, filled our Christmas holidays. Xmas is essentially a nostalgic event, a celebration of nostalgia: for snow, for childhood for Ladybird Books and Spirographs, for maps of the world coloured mainly red, for winter evenings in the firelight, snow falling and notes sent up the chimney to the household deity, who may be seen to represent the spirits of the dead and to be drawn from folk-beliefs dating back to the pre-Christian era. I am nostalgic for reel-to-reel tapes and the first hit singles of The Beatles. The New Youth of the Rock Generation has done something in American popular song that has been begged to be done for generations. Sing me a song from a dream, a song from another world, the world of dream, which some say is a parallel universe, a shadow or distorted mirror of the waking world, others say is a bizarre and meaningless show, caused by the reordering of data and chemical balances in the brain. My dream was of a small boy I remember, stock-still, as he kept his distance from the other lives. He didn't join in, that morning, with those who played in the trees to multiply the universe. As for American popular song, it has taken the creation of the lyrics and the music out of the hands of the hacks and given it over to the poets.

48.

The sound of rain on the leaves is exact and full of meaning. It means leaves in rain, rain attending to its native qualities, taking meaning from the phrase 'rain on the leaves', taking presence from the meaning of an opening time presents through a window that lets in cool air, fine spray, a sound of wet branches brushing against the wall, the drip and steady patter, and again, swish of branches; like sea-sound, but nowhere near any sea. The rain, the rain itself that is, is exact and native to its qualities, meaning a phrase, an opening, a presence other than cool air, rain-drip, sea-sound simile, wall, and open window. It comes from some place that is no place other than this one. Cases have been recorded of people who (by ordinary standards) forgot so little that their everyday activities were full of confusion. There's no forgetting the present. The present is leaves in rain, taking meaning from the phrase 'rain on the leaves' set down here in the present of these words. Set down while trying to concentrate on the present. Why try to concentrate on it? What else is there to be aware of? Your memories are all in the present, just as much as those trees over there. As much as leaves in rain. Memory, that's what we are, our lives, our identity, all made of memory. Try forgetting, then see what happens. It is more like stumbling into a clearing in the forest, where suddenly you can move and see clearly.

Through effort we develop our character. In this hexagram, wood, standing for our character, nourishes fire; through the good example of our character, we light the way for others. This gives meaning to our lives. At fifty, a man should be rich. But how many are? Money isn't the answer—it's transient and unworthy of our attention. The life span of a five-pound note is one year on average. Between 2004 and 2005, the Bank of England reported that 153,531,778 five-pound notes were shredded. Lakshmi Mittal, aged 55, is the richest man in Britain, with an estimated fortune of 14.9 billion pounds derived from his steel empire. But is he happy? My daughter, born Nottingham 1996, passes me a note: Dad please come up in 15 minutes with water and a Nerofen. I know this is a wrong spelling SOS. The phone is ringing. Hello? It's my mother, born Newcastle-upon-Tyne 1923. She's had a slight fall and spent the afternoon in casualty, but sounds OK now. Now it's time to settle my daughter down in bed. A glass of water and some Nurofen. And I've caught a cold. If I were rich, these things would still happen. We light the way for others. This gives meaning to our lives. My father, born Newcastle-upon-Tyne 1921, died, Newcastle-upon-Tyne 1973, has nothing to say; yet his influence at this time is propitious, and worth more, I may say, than all the banknotes shredded by the Bank of England. And he wasn't rich, or anything like it, at fifty.

As if this place were a dream of this place, that comes from no where other than here. If this were true, then ducks rising from a pond in a flurry and splash are taking off into a season of late promise, into which, while the power station spreads its clouds (which, incidentally, are mainly water vapour), late developers come to skinny-dip and young women dream of men who make them laugh. For the young, all things are possible. Would you like to reconsider? The tapestries tell of meadow flowers and men with lutes that strolled through the young land like news of peace, mixed with the uncomfortable freedom that peace brings. The word troubadour is a French form derived ultimately from the Occitanian trobar, 'to find' or 'to invent'. A troubadour was thus one who invented new poems, finding new verse for his elaborate love lyrics. The young girl in love invents her lover anew, perhaps while lighting a cigarette or texting her friend. The mind thus invents a place that is no where else than the place it's in; the ducks are in full flight now, the estuary extends, painterly and complete, under an extravagant sky. Meanwhile, Super Mario clears the way to a lower (indestructible) floor and heads to the first pipe spawning Bobombs. If you've forgotten your password, we can send it to you by email. A home without books is like a room without windows. The casement swung open and she leaned into the May morning, hoping this wasn't a dream.

If the kingdom of the stars seems vast, the realm of the galaxies is larger still. From the North Devon coast we could see the Welsh Hills across the sea, and when night fell, the Milky Way was a pale crystal band across the sky. Our home galaxy is a large spiral system consisting of several billion stars, one of which is the Sun. Many such assemblages are so enormous that they contain hundreds of billions of stars. And yet there are so many galaxies that they pervade space, even into the depths of the farthest reaches penetrated by powerful modern telescopes. Look, I said, if you lie on the grass out here you can see the Milky Way. They rolled their eyes and smiled at each other, but came anyway. The stars were like jewels in a black roof. Below the cliff, we heard sea-surf sounding. At dawn the tides withdraw, currents pull round the headland to the grey Atlantic, past Lundy Island, where seals stare like the souls of the drowned. To have a soul would mean that consciousness was separate from the physical body. Every visible star is a sun in its own right. Ever since this realization first dawned in the collective mind of humanity, it has been speculated that many stars other than the Sun also have planetary systems encircling them, and that some will have life, even advanced civilizations. For the early Egyptians, the Milky Way was the heavenly Nile, flowing through the land of the dead ruled by Osiris.

There's a fine drizzle falling outside. This is not a diary. But what is it? Is there a rain falling? Is it outside? We should ask the scientists; they are the intellectual elite, the brains the rest of us rely on to make sense of the universe and answer the big questions. But in a refreshing show of New Year humility, the world's best thinkers have admitted that from time to time even they are forced to change their minds. At the time of writing the above words, it was certainly raining outside, but at the time of writing these ones, it isn't, and the rain is a memory, certainly here in the present, but in a modified form. Tonight I may dream about it. When we dream and when we couple, we embrace phantoms. There is neither form nor presence: there is the wave that rocks us, the gallop across the plains of night. Get better soon. As for the difference between SoCal and England, well, Kathy's been sick too, for a couple weeks now ... with a virus. But there probably is more sunshine here ... Which is why the sky and the light often loom large in my poems ... Night and the winter solstice loom large here. We live in night with cloudy interludes. I still have the slip of paper she wrote her phone number on, after all this time. I couldn't believe my luck, still can't. Eroticism ... is a thirst for otherness. And the supernatural is the supreme otherness.

[He] remembered not only every leaf of every tree of every wood, but also every one of the times he had perceived or imagined it. Forgetfulness might seem bliss, like falling asleep in a comfortable bed after physical work in the fresh air. If you find that difficult, it's something that can be learned. Simple breathing exercises can help, or meditation. Some people find that lavender oil, valerian or other herbs help them. In a prose piece, he envisages a School of Forgetting, where the pupils are taught in specialist fields, such as Forgetting History and Forgetting Language. In the lit room, the window pane is a black square, the streaks of rain are like little lines of glass beads. The modem is flickering, the printer is warming up. There is the case of 'AJ', a 40-year-old woman with incredibly strong memories of her personal past. Given a date, AJ can recall with astonishing accuracy what she was doing on that date and what day of the week it fell on. Because her case is the first one of its kind, the researchers have proposed a name for her syndrome—'hyperthymestic syndrome'. She had been called 'the human calendar' for years by her friends and acquaintances. AJ is both a warden and a prisoner of her memories, said Parker, a clinical professor of psychiatry and neurology. They can at times be a burden because they cannot be controlled, but she told us that if she had a choice, she would not want to give them up.

54.

Synchronicity takes the coincidence of events in space and time as meaning something more than mere chance. The observer and the observed are in reciprocal dependence. But who observes the observers? Oscar died after his Honda Accord crossed into oncoming traffic on Highway 99 near Yuba City. California Highway Patrol officers found that the computer consultant's laptop was plugged into the car's cigarette lighter ... I go downstairs, walk into the living room and sit down. On TV a man wears a concealed earpiece and must follow instructions relayed through it by another man, a 'celebrity' who is hidden. The man is told to say embarrassing things, to make inappropriate gestures, to get down and walk on all fours, like a dog. This hexagram reflects a situation in which any movement makes matters worse. It is useless to think on why we are in the situation, or toward getting out of it; all energy must be put toward relating properly until we are out of danger. I had a headache this afternoon which made me have to sit on a darkened room clutching my face. Not nice. Thank god for painkillers. When the headache subsided I lay there remembering the small house I grew up in, at the edge of fields with a view of the Cheviot hills. We moved there one midsummer, during those almost eerie light evenings. Sometimes I think all the holidays I take, often in small cottages or chalets, are an attempt to re-create that world, which is a world invented in retrospect.

The fifty-sixth hexagram: in the inner universe, we are wanderers and strangers. In the list of *1001 Books to Read Before You Die*, I have read seventy-five. But have I? Some I've listened to, some I read many years ago but can no longer remember (though still claim to have read them). When it was announced that the Library contained all books, the first reaction was unbounded joy. Reading was a form of remembering, more reliable than the real thing, because you were under no illusions that what was reconstructed was an actual event, but a virtual one. Memory itself entails misperceptions of all sorts, partly corrected, bringing rare moments of joy by the faculty of 'involuntary' memory. These moments of connection with the past are brought about by contingent encounters in the present, which re-awaken long-lost sensations, perceptions and recollections. The road runs between dune and dune, down to an expanse where flocks of tern scattered at our coming, and that soon the tide's fathoms will return to Cuthbert's creatures, seal and shoal. Then, an island will be born, or re-born in the brighter element of sky and sea. I was a school-kid, drinker, father, husband, worker; but who were those people? Where are they now? We are wanderers and strangers. I'd forget my own name if it wasn't on my lapel badge next to the corporate logo. Mission statement: to find the central path through avoiding indulgence and mortification. To read the *Daily Mirror* sports pages less often. To create a way of awakening.

I dreamt I was walking at night along a wide road near the docks of a Baltic town. The road was deserted, the wind was cold, I was just walking, walking, there was no end to it. I awoke in a small hotel room in a Baltic town and lay listening to the wind. At Choice hotels, we don't want all our hotels to look alike and provide identical experiences. We want our customers to have choices, which is why our company is called 'Choice'. In the dream, I had no choice. I was just walking, walking, and I didn't know who I was. I didn't know I was the person who typed this text. The voices of the writing do not 'frame' a personality in the sense of making it possible to reconstruct that as a cohesive whole. Notice also, despite its diversity and complexity, how the world is always present in a way that makes sense. Let's consult the *Sunday Mirror*: Yummy mummy Davina McCall is feeling sexier than ever as she shows off her curves in a stunning satin dress. 'Fifteen months after having our son Chester, I'm feeling hornier than ever. It's like we're having a renaissance'. When we couple, we embrace phantoms. There is neither form nor presence. Nothing ever stands still—keep moving ahead with us. Keep walking along the wide, deserted road, the wind blowing from the Baltic, there'll be a dream waiting for you at the end of your sleep. It'll be like you're having a renaissance.

The process of filling in the bay had been going on for one hundred years. The reduced market for egg-hatching machines and spittle-cups made the change necessary. Whatever its appeal, Malmo is full of funkiness. People don't usually hang out in restaurants till late in the evening and it can be hard, thus, to track down a decent meal after dark should you get famished in the wee hours. The taxi took me down a dark road, far away from where I wanted to go, finally leaving me at a deserted hotel with no obvious way back. I had no choice but to climb the steps to the poorly lit lobby. Death is no longer enshrined in taboos. What was this hotel? My reflection in the doorway revealed to me my true self: a bipedal primate mammal, anatomically related to the great apes but distinguished by a more highly developed brain, with a resultant capacity for articulate speech and abstract reasoning, and by a marked erectness of body carriage that frees the hands for use as manipulative members. Famished in the wee hours. Burnt out on the trail. Not using my modem (I get no dial tone). A haunted man. Then she uprose, the only rose for me. She didn't understand me, nor I her, but that made things more interesting. She knew that the moon influenced the cycle of the tides. She circumnavigated the globe, she shook my pockets loose and took me home to meet my life. My hands were freed as manipulative members.

58.

The January sky was pale blue, with watery clouds. My perception of the world is limited by my five senses, and my perception of image is limited by my sensual perception of light. Image, time, mind and memory … to try to capture them seems absurd and futile. When my grandfather was out of work, he'd scrub the kitchen floor; he was a good man, my mother tells me. He fell out of an army truck and escaped the Great War. My perception of him is limited by my five senses. He is here in the present, along with my entire past, this desk and computer, along also with the future. The history and energy of presence. Good night, see you in the morning—that's the kids sorted out, let's have a glass of wine. The present, singular or plural, pale as January's sky with all its clouds. The past is present like a shifting sky of pale blue and thin cloud. The future, all our futures, are a presence like a shifting blue in a cloudy sky. All futures are invented. The origin of futures was in trade in agricultural commodities, and the term is used to define the underlying asset even though the contract is frequently completely divorced from the product. As you age, your future contracts. I see the future without me in it—with my children in it maybe. Nothing ever stands still—keep moving ahead with us. The future is orange. The future doesn't exist. Let's pour the wine.

Children today learn about sex, gunslinging, drug dealing and other forms of corruption much earlier than their parents did, but they learn very little about death. Halloween is based on a medieval European concept of death, and is populated by demons, witches (usually women) and other images of terror—all of them negative. The Day of the Dead, in contrast, is distinctly different, and demonstrates a strong sense of love and respect for one's ancestors. The souls of the dead return each year to visit with their living relatives—to eat, drink and be merry. Just like they did when they were living. Today I got news from my mother that my uncle Joe has died. In what seems like another age I was playing in front of the open fire when my mam called from the kitchen 'Come and see your Uncle Joe.' I ran in to see, sitting on a chair in the middle of the little scullery, an apparition, an impossibly tall, angular man wreathed in clouds of cigarette smoke, smiling down at me. When somebody close to us dies, there follows a time of great sadness, with many preparations needing to be made for the organising of a funeral. funeralsuk.com is here to help you with the arranging and planning. Rain, fog and gales are playing their usual part in the January weather, but with the compensation of winter light, when crisp air and the sun low in the sky combine to form a brightness beyond the reach of summer.

60.

At family gatherings Uncle Joe would stand with his back to the fire, tall, garrulous, smiling, breaking into song, cigar and whisky in hand, a benevolent if slightly authoritarian figure. As of Sunday, he's no longer with us. As sub prime is a growing section of the mortgage market, it has been identified as an area in which the FSA should assess the appropriateness of advised sales. My manager is making my life very stressful. It's not personal. Is it? I'll maintain my Buddhist calm and detachment—that should annoy the bastard. The plural pleasures pass at pace the pleasures of singularity. I should remember that when I just want everyone to leave me alone. Do not live in unawareness. Do not embrace false views. I have spoken to families who have lost their credit, their home, their dignity and even their jobs. After that, what's left? By late 2007, one in ten homes in Cleveland had been repossessed and Deutsche Bank Trust, acting on behalf of bondholders, was the largest property owner in the city. Hey Dad, could you give me a lift to Sophie's house? I think she sees me as a tall, smiling, benevolent if slightly authoritarian figure. Under the blue sky in the bright sunlight you don't have to point out this and that any more. But the causal conditions of time and seasons still require you to give the medicine in accordance with the disease. Tell me, is it better to let go or is it better to hold on?

Of all Charles Dickens' novels, *Middlemarch* is the one I like best: 'Who that cares much to know the history of man, and how the mysterious mixture behaves under the varying experiments of Time'. Things I have to do: research into buying a new car (ours has done 88,000 miles), book a holiday before the cheap deals get snapped up, send a sympathy card for Uncle Joe, email Clive, get my haircut, remember my father thirty years dead (he got on well with Joe). When I was a child adults praised me for my curiosity. Now, other adults think I am a curiosity, at least when I tell them I'm a poet. Also, buy envelopes, book a dentist's appointment. Time: a measured or measurable period, a continuum that lacks spatial dimensions. Time is of philosophical interest and is also the subject of mathematical and scientific investigation. It's the element in which we live. My memory, sir, is like a garbage heap … I think of my father, thirty years dead. The road runs between dune and dune, down to an expanse where flocks of tern scattered at our coming. Taking that road, running down the dune to the sea with my brother and sister—what was I doing? Creating myself, that I'm re-creating now. It's as if our whole consciousness is constructed from the past. Nevertheless, there is indeed a more prolonged psychological present, a brief period during which successive events seem to form a perceptual unity and can be apprehended without calling on memory.

The character called Kî is used as a symbol of being past or completed. Žî denotes primarily crossing a stream, and has the secondary meaning of helping and completing. The two characters, combined, will express the successful accomplishment of whatever the writer has in his mind. What do I have in my mind? 1. The noise of the Wii console which the girls are playing in the next room. 2. An anxiety due to writing this instead of working (this is a 'working from home' day). 3. I must book that week at Centre Parcs. Thus we behave under the varying experiments of Time, which once again has got me leaning on the window sill looking into the dusk, trying to make out some figures across the park. Who are they? What are they doing? Sounds of a fiddle being played and the long twilight make the streetlights seem impossibly remote. There they are again, those figures in the half-light, not menacing, but strange. Only the barking dogs break the spell that spells disaster, but there's no need to take them too seriously, and anyway, disaster is my meat and drink. Still, I wish they'd take their leave with whatever rituals and exaggerated farewells are needed. The fiddle, or is it in fact an old and expensive violin, sounds, I can only say, strange. Then follows hexagram Fû, belonging to the eleventh month, in which was mid-winter's day, when the sun turned back in his course, and moved with a constant regular progress towards the summer solstice.

Hexagram sixty-four, 'crossing the great water', means getting past a period which is dangerous to our perseverance. It's time to book a holiday. I logged off and slipped out of the office through the side entrance. I walked out into the morning, along the bank of the swollen river, unaccountably happy. When crossing a river, don't get your tail wet (the sixty-fourth hexagram warns against this). It's usually cheaper to book flight and accommodation separately. I'm looking for somewhere with almond trees and evergreen oak above a carpet of flowers, terraced hillsides with cedars and a coastal path to the moorish watchtower, a 'view over the bay'. We went horse riding on a trail through the hills; I guess these things invoke some collective memory of a nomadic past. I took books on poetics and psychology (she said 'they're a bit heavy, here's a magazine' and I never read the books). Te-shan rode up in his cart with his notes on the *Diamond Sutra* and right in front of the Zen hall he built a big fire with them saying, 'Even though you have exhausted the abstruse doctrines, it's like placing a hair in vast estates. Even though you have learned all the secrets of the world, it's like letting a single drop of water fall into an enormous valley'. And he burned up all his notes. He walked out into the morning, along the bank of the swollen river, unaccountably happy, replete with the compensation of winter light, a brightness beyond the reach of summer.

EVERYDAY SONGS

DRIVING SONGS

possible worlds
revolve on the ring-road
between gear changes
and ferocious word-play

unprecedented steps
by the Bank of England
what time will I get home
to revive the economy

though he wonders
when he'll see
his family again, yet
the stars are grinning

in a speculative
but benevolent way,
watching his lonely progress
through the dancing traffic

roadworks on the M5
occasional sun,
the foreign secretary
being inflammatory

cows flashing
past, the day brightening,
thoughts straggling
the structure of the brain

how much petrol's left
and is desperately sorry
and happy by turns,
in Limbo or the Elysian fields

in the green and pleasant
not one to spoil things,
but, of course,
there is no 'present moment'

I knew it was time
to stir, to set out
in midsomer seson
of high, green corn

to the slip-road
of the widened M1
in search of tree-dwellers
and traffic-calming measures

when my country
into which I had just
set foot, was set on
fire about mine ears,

when memory gave us
the elbow, it was
time to stir. It was
time for every man to stir

there's a ghost
of a narrative,
stalking all the cars,
sudden tail-lights

coming back
after visiting relatives
starlings in the dusk …
Israel vows

twisting, curling,
moving as one
in the red sunset …
to continue its offensive

a huge swarm in the sky
as night falls
we won't raise
the white flag

Tel Aviv says it 'may'
have used white phosphorus
guardian angels, whirlwinds
the wrath of time

but only, and again
these men and women
struggled and sacrificed
and worked till

their hands were raw
so that we might live
a better this
is the new machine

swept on sheen of early,
clean morning, a bee
banging into the windscreen
trying to enter the world's reflection.

out on the road
in an effortless
lyrical, narrative impulse
here, and not-here

the stars climb more easily
than I do, than signals
from the war on terror,
the violence in the night sky

o open the window, can you see
'these elaborately constructed forms
so different from each other
and dependent on each

other in so a complex manner'
read all about it
among a glut of new works
on the great naturalist

the near explains the far
the drop is a small ocean
the wind is blowing
litter in little circles

and a woman is walking
down the road
with two small children
past people waiting for a bus

I went to the woods
because I wished to live
deliberately / the litter
blows in circles

the wind in the trees
looks like a 'dance of life',
a cliché, but that's how it looks,
through the windscreen

apparently off-hand,
slip-shod or casual,
the bulletins crafted
from the finest propaganda

wave like trees
on the ridge,
presenting a vision
of England's diaspora

adapted for us like
the slip-shod glow
of finest vision
20-20 prime-time

crafted casually
by revenue and region
the bottom-line laid
like a line of pentameter

The wind always blows
let it take whatever it can
of time, river traffic
in the sun, alone

among many, or
the story of a better life,
of morning
open to the city,

river traffic,
field of sky,
field of water,
field of, and city

we may call it
a book of shadows,
'quantitative easing'
last throw of the dice

traffic in the sun,
windy tower blocks, swaying
grasses on the edge of the road,
the voices of girls in thin dresses

drifting into the dusk
of the shortest day.
Travelodge is here
to make you feel better off.

Things can only get longer
for the waifs who stray
through the retail park
lights on 24/7

to the global window
opening on their lives.
I'd like en suite bathroom,
food and beverage options.

KITCHEN SONGS

familial memories,
displacement and diaspora,
a weave of years
wrapped around the self

to keep the night cold
distant, as the kitchen
at the end
of day cools

crowded with emptiness,
illegible, warm
with longing and
submerged commentaries

that say change
must soon come
over to the window
there are faces in the street

the walkers are walking
their dogs in the dusk,
the park is a fair
field full of folk

and such is the irresistible
nature of truth,
that all it asks,
and all it wants

is the liberty of appearing
in justice and plain dealing
not king-waste and delusion,
England's lamentable slaverie

the kettle's boiled,
the shops are open,
the street-lights are shining
in the english night

this is the world machine
working in pale winter
green, but not much green
in cars and shopping bags

and how many meetings does it
take to leave work early
and earn the pleasure
of listening to the radio

in a cold kitchen
preparing food
and waiting for the kids
to come home from school

turning the volume down
but still hearing the Archbishop
and the Knight of the Realm
spinning fairy stories

events are sensational
and continuous,
accumulating complexly
layered patterns

of sound and sense
arranged around echoes
in a world where
the youngest child's ill

and we wait in A&E
for seven hours
and we long
for the green world again

that in the morning
might be in the
morning might
be ours again

the baffled king composing
hallelujah in the charts
turn the radio up
then off, the field

is so bright this afternoon
would anyone turn it down?
I would, I would
consult the scattered sticks,

the dice, the hand of cards
dealt with all the luxury
of rhythmic colour and
the magic that spells a new era

listening to the speech:
government of the people—
click here for all you need—
shall not perish from the earth

I'd like to use
repetition, pace,
tone, voice changes
and delay

to make new
emphases, ordered
rankings or dimensions,
I'd like to chant

with the grasses
on Clifton ridge,
in somer seson
of low inflation

when the corn is green
and my house open
to the trade winds
dressed in newsprint

clean trees of winter
washed of colour
against a starry blue sky
present an ambitious whole

are you at home
among the fluid selves
and shifting
unstable texts?

are we at home
in the questionable winter
twilight speaking
disjunctive sentences

startling imagery
and meditations on art,
reality, and whether
it's time for another cup of tea?

cycles and seasons
The Cloudspotter's Guide
the blu-ray store,
the January sale

the 4 for 3 offer
and white phosphorus
fired into narrow streets
and crowded alleyways

The world.
Say it again. It's
what we think with,
traversing the network

inventing every scene
'man, the language animal'
building conceptual structures
in several dimensions

look at the trees
waving in the morning—
are they celebratory
critical, defiant

or open-hearted?
Their very existence
raises a question which,
together, we might decipher

while people set out for work
dawdling schoolchildren
push each other off the pavement,
and the clouds

whose power to determine
the day's outcome
is considerable, leave
a message on the empty sky

high water's rising everywhere
in this song,
a constant calm
and searching among vocabularies

and scattered books
on the floor.
There would be music
in this scene

curtains drawn and tiny
openings for being that ask for
'quiet on the set'. Listen:
there's a disturbing lyricism at work

a friend bringing
unexpected morning coffee
as if to say
there's a way of writing about hope

READING SONGS

I've been battered by
intellectual awe and
erotic surrender, the knife,
the clouds, a harvest

fruit and tender ironies,
need, and various births
so put the book down,
sip my tea, listen for sounds

in the empty room
cool but bright afternoon
the whole of my life
and my sum of experience

is the sound of a dog
barking in the distance
and clouds
passing quickly

so return
to a seductively-paced
travelogue—both exotic
and erotic, neurotic

not psychotic,
the geography of flesh
on the bone, the challenge
of 'otherness' still remains

receiving radio transmissions
from outer space
or the state of mind
induced by consumption

translations of absent bodies,
the impossible quest
for the self, the hope
for an end to hostilities

it's hard associating
arbitrary names (or symbols)
with memory locations
to interpret a series

of mnemonics that correspond
to a stream of executable
instructions bringing dukka/anguish/
suffering to an end

according to the
eight-fold path
yet suffering, is
relative, the news says

ceasefire holding
residents surveying
the wreckage, returning
to what's left of home

a work of complex
sensuousness and deeply
intelligent, unobtrusive
air attacks, meditative lyricism

almost painterly
precision bombing
implodes gracefully
sideways at our lives

scattering petals
on the wet branches
and then we ask
if there's more to things

than this uncertainty
than this mess
that only lives through us
and our story-telling

a wondrous book
of parables, meditative
cantos, interstices
between ourselves

casting Zen-like nets
and a friend has sent
me a book called anxiety
chant and I'm reading

this town / and others /
empty / of boxes and lives /
in yellow light /
coats the empty room

and thinking counter-music
of fluid selves,
ethical, aesthetic
and full of ideals

astounded at
a different taste
and texture, rhythm
and judicious pause

the poet bringing
together abstraction
and precise images
to explore

the intensities
the contraries
of lyric thinking,
and reversals

the proximity
of 870 job-losses
of difference
of being safe-at-home

read brightly, with fine
economy and precision,
speak incantations
in a pace we can keep up with

what we need is fierce
indignation and
the wrath of ... writes Geoffrey
in knotty verse

meanwhile the hungry
and disadvantaged
starlings scour the field
in skipping groups

offering different angles
on the social network
and a multi-dimensional
measured response

I'm reading about
contemporary Glasgow
filtered through the mesh
of a Chinese martial-arts movie

of an increasingly
dystopian terrain
cleaved, divided
against herself, delivering

the presence of an ancient,
rotting city,
openings through place
into mystery. Eden poised

against a world of political
and historical change.
Crumbled Raj-world.
The mid-world of England.

Refracting ordinary light
into acute images,
drawing upon jazz clubs
in empty cotton warehouses

a rich, lucid prose inviting
comparisons, inhabiting
Cambridge pubs,
embracing non-sequiturs

and apparently-random
thoughts. The presence
of an ancient
rotting city. The idea

of heavenly music
A palimpsest where
edges are blurred
and erased.

I read the world
then closed its
pages. I held
the text of

false memory, thanks.
I'd like to say
that valuable lessons
have been learnt.

Phenomena noted.
All the places of home
defamiliarized
to otherwhere

with great precision,
seeming at once stable
and highly unstable, where
much is fluid, shifting and uneasy.

NOTES

NOT BONDI BEACH

Chilwell: Most of the shells used by the British artillery in the Battle of the Somme were produced at an industrial plant grafted onto the tiny Nottinghamshire village of Chilwell. Local people used the smaller shell-cases as vases for flowers.

A Darkened Country: The epigraph is from John Bunyan's *Pilgrim's Progress*.

THE STRANGE CITY

Joseph Wright of Derby lived 1734-1797. The best collection of his paintings is in Derby Museum and Art Gallery.

THE BOOK OF RANDOM ACCESS

Most of the words are 'my own', including quotations from poems I had written previously, but much of the text is constructed from quotations from the following sources:

1.   p. 89
The Encyclopedia Britannica entry on 'Time'
Wikipedia entry on 'Time'
Carole K. Anthony, *A Guide to the I Ching* (Anthony Publishing, 1980)
Notes to John Bloomberg-Rissman, *No Sounds of My Own Making* (Leafe Press, 2007)

2.   p. 90
Encyclopedia Britannica entry on 'Memory'
Anthony, *A Guide to the I Ching*
Geshe Kelsang Gyatso, *The Meditation Handbook* (Tharpa Publications, 1993)

3.   p. 91

F. T. Prince, introduction to *Comus and Other Poems* by John Milton
(Oxford University Press, 1968)
'I might perhaps leave something so written ...', John Milton, *The
Reason of Church Government Urged Against Prelaty* (1642)
Stephen Batchelor, *Buddhism Without Beliefs: A Contemporary Guide to
Awakening* (Bloomsbury, 1997)

4.   p. 92

Alan Watts, *In My Own Way: An Autobiography 1915-1965* (Vintage
1973)

5.   p. 93

Oral testimony from my mother, Mrs M. Forster, formerly Baker, née
Bowman (born 1923, Newcastle-upon-Tyne)
'The Keel Row': traditional Tyneside song, adopted by the military
as a marching song.
Milton's sonnet 'How Soon Hath Time'

6.   p. 94

Introductory booklet, The Oral History Society (2007)
Jane Renouf, 'The Way We Were', compiled from interviews made
by Ambleside Oral History Group, originally published in *The
Westmorland Gazette* (1987)
Anthony, *A Guide to the I Ching*
The Dhammapada, trans. Narada Thera (Buddha Educational
Foundation, 1963)

7.   p. 95

Nicholas Rogers, *Halloween: From Pagan Ritual to Party Night* (Oxford
University Press, 2003)
Wikipedia entry on 'Time'
Paul Simon, 'America' (1968)
The Rolling Stones, 'Paint it Black' (1966)

W. S. Graham, 'Of the Resonant Rumour of Sun, Impulse of Summer' (1942)

8. p. 96
Yves Bonnefoy, *Début et Fin de la Neige* (Mercure de France, 1991), trans. Alan Baker
Anthony, *A Guide to the I Ching*
Marcel Proust, *Swann's Way*, trans. C. K. Scott Moncrieff (1922)

9. p. 97
Bonnefoy, *Début et Fin de la Neige*
Padraic Colum, introduction, *The Complete Grimm's Fairy Tales* (Random House, 1980)
'The Moon', *The Complete Grimm's Fairy Tales*

10. p. 98
Edmond Jabès, *The Book of Questions*, trans. Rosemary Waldrop (Wesleyan University Press, 1991)
Henri Bergson, *The Creative Mind: An Introduction to Metaphysics*, trans. Mabell L. Andison (Citadel, 1992)

12. p. 100
'My Bonny Lad': traditional Tyneside song

14. p. 102
<http://orientalpearls.blogspot.com/>
Sir Walter Ralegh, 'His Pilgrimage' (c. 1603)

15. p. 103
Paul Simon, 'Another Galaxy' (2006)
Anthony, *A Guide to the I Ching*
'On this day in 1985', news.bbc.co.uk/, 3 March 2005
Jean Spence and Carol Stephenson, 'Female Involvement in the Miner's Strike 1984-1985: Trajectories of Activism', *Sociological Research Online*, vol 12, issue 1 (2007)

16.   p. 104

J. M. Synge, *The Aran Islands* (1907)
Anthony, *A Guide to the I Ching*
Robert Burns, 'Lassie, Lie Near Me' (1790)
Oral testimony of my mother
Gabriel Yacoub, 'Les choses les plus simple', performed by June Tabor, *At the Woods Heart* (Topic, 2005)

17.   p. 105

Encyclopedia Britannica entry on 'Relativity'

19.   p. 107

Encyclopedia Britannica entry on 'Relativity'

20.   p. 108

Encyclopedia Britannica entry on 'Time'

21.   p. 109

Encyclopedia Britannica entries on 'Quantum Mechanics' and 'Uncertainty Theory'

22.   p. 110

Anthony, *A Guide to the I Ching*
Zen koan from the *Gendai Sōjizen Hoyōron*, trans. Yoel Hoffmann, *The Sound of One Hand: 281 Zen Koans with Answers* (Basic Books, 1975)

23.   p. 111

Anthony, *A Guide to the I Ching*
Quotation from Lama Zopa Rinpoche

24.   p. 112

Batchelor, *Buddhism Without Beliefs*

25.   p. 113

Charlotte Brontë on Jane Austen

National Trust Handbook 2007, on Hardwick Hall and Sudbury Hall, Derbyshire

The Proceedings of the Old Bailey: London's Central Criminal Court, 1674-1913 (<http://www.oldbaileyonline.org/>)

26.   p. 114

Newcastle Evening Chronicle, 19 November 2007

Renouf, 'The Way We Were'

Spence and Stephenson, 'Female Involvement in the Miner's Strike'

Encyclopedia Britannica entry on 'Collective Unconsciousness'

27.   p. 115

Syd Barrett, 'Chapter 24' (1967)

28.   p. 116

Carl Jung, *Memories, Dreams, Reflections*, trans. Richard and Clara Winston (Pantheon Books, 1963)

Letter from Her Majesty's Revenue and Customs to 7.5 million families in the UK

29.   p. 117

Carling beer advertisement

Wikipedia entry on 'Beer'

Oral testimony of my mother

30.   p. 118

Encyclopedia Britannica entries on 'Memory Abnormality' and 'Virtual Memory (Computer Science)'

Samuel Taylor Coleridge, 'The Rime of the Ancient Mariner' (1798)

31.   p. 119
Wikipedia entry on 'Holocene Period'
Glossary of Imporant Terms in Glacial Geology, Monatana
State University (<http://www.homepage.montana.edu/~geol445/
hyperglac/glossary.htm>)

32.   p. 120
The Guardian, 1 November 2007
UK Health and Safety Executive (<http://www.hse.gov.uk/stress/>)

33.   p. 121
Emails from John Bloomberg-Rissman and Kris Hemensley
Edmond Jabès, *The Book of Shares*, trans. Rosemary Waldrop
(University of Chicago Press, 1989)
'Language is the new Spiritus Mundi'!: Marjorie Perloff, quoted in
Recalling and Rereading Edmond Jabès by Rosemary Waldrop (Wesleyan
University Press, 2002)

34.   p. 122
Proust, *Swann's Way*

35.   p. 123
Encyclopedia Britannica entry on 'Snow'
François Villon, 'Ballade des dames du temps jadis'

36.   p. 124
J. H. Prynne, review of *Response to Futures* by Ken Edwards, *Golden
Handcuffs Review*, vol. 1, no. 9 (Winter-Spring 2007-2008)

37.   p. 125
'The Battle of Otterburn' (early 16th century): a Border Ballad
James Reed, introduction, *Border Ballads: A Selection* (Carcanet, 1991)

Prynne, review of *Response to Futures*
Wikipedia entry on 'UK Miners Strike (1984-1985)'

38.   p. 126
Notes on the Miners Strike, 1984-1985 (<http://libcom.org/library/notes-on-the-miners-strike-1984-1985/>)
Encyclopedia Britannica entries on 'Snow' and 'Ice'

39.   p. 127
Encyclopedia Britannica entries on 'Taoism' and '*I Ching*'

40.   p. 128
Encyclopedia Britannica entry on 'Wernicke's Aphasia'
Bill Griffiths, 'The Green Man Reconsidered'
<http://www.trustedreviews.com/apple/review>

41.   p. 129
Hugh R. Trevor-Roper, *The European Witch-Craze of the 16th and 17th Centuries* (Penguin, 1969)

42.   p. 130
Encyclopedia Britannica entries on 'Halloween' and 'Life'

43.   p. 131
Coca Cola advertisement
Encyclopedia Britannica entry on 'Life'
Ian Brinton, review of *Wolf Tongue: Selected Poems 1965-2000* by Barry MacSweeney, *Litter* (2007)
David Caddy, 'Poetic Letters from England, Letter 8' (2007) (<http://davidcaddy.blogspot.com/2007/12/letter-8.html>)

44.   p. 132
Encyclopedia Britannica entries on 'Halloween' and 'Taoism'
Gyatso, *The Meditation Handbook*

46.   p. 134

Interview with Dr. Michio Kaku, BBC

M. R. Franks, *The Universe and Multiple Reality: A Physical Explanation for Manifesting Magick and Miracles* (iUniverse, 2003)

P. C. W. Davies and J. R. Brown, eds. *The Ghost in the Atom: A Discussion of the Mysteries of Quantum Physics* (Cambridge University Press, 1986)

Sir James Jeans, *The Mysterious Universe*, 2nd ed. (Cambridge University Press, 1932)

47.   p. 135

Bishop Boniface on the Venerable Bede

Coleridge, 'The Rime of the Ancient Mariner'

48.   p. 136

Julie Lumsden, 'Rheindalen' from *Naked by Profession* (Leafe Press, 2000)

Ralph J. Gleason, liner notes to *Parsley, Sage, Rosemary and Thyme* by Simon and Garfunkel (1966)

50.   p. 138

Anthony, *A Guide to the I Ching*

Ben Schott, *Schott's Almanac 2007* (Bloomsbury, 2006)

51.   p. 139

Encyclopedia Britannica entry on 'Troubadour'

Slogan from Jacqueline Wilson's website (<http://www.jacqueline wilson.co.uk/>)

New Super Mario Brothers Cheats (<http://www.cheatscodesguides. com/>)

52.   p. 140

Encyclopedia Britannica entries on 'Galaxy' and 'Cosmos'

53. p. 141

The Guardian, 6 January 2001

Email from John Bloomberg-Rissman

54. p. 142

Jorge Luis Borges, 'Funes the Memorious' from *Labyrinths* (1962)

'Hyper Memory: The Inability to Forget', BrainMind.com News (7 March 2006) (<http://www.brainmind.com/memoryhyper. html>)

Dennis Tomlinson, review of *The Nightingale Question: 5 Poets from Saxony*, ed. and trans. Tessa Ransford, *Tears in the Fence* 46 (2007)

55. p. 143

Anthony, *A Guide to the I Ching*

The Darwin Awards 2007 (<http://www.darwinawards.com/>)

56. p. 144

Sarah Dillon, review of *À la Recherche du Temps Perdu* by Marcel Proust, *1001 Books to Read Before You Die* (Cassel, 2007)

Borges, *Labyrinths*

57. p. 145

The Sunday Mirror, 6 January 2008

Choice Hotels marketing brochure

Leslie Scalapino, introduction to *Overtime: Selected Poems* by Philip Whalen (Penguin, 1999)

58. p. 146

Encyclopedia Britannica entries on 'Death' and 'Human Being'

59. p. 147

Encyclopedia Britannica entry on 'Futures'

Eric Gamalinda, 'Language, Light and the Language of Light', *Pinoy Poetics: A Collection of Autobiographical and Critical Essays on Filipino and Filipino-American Poetics*, ed. Nick Carbo (Meritage Press, 2004)

60.   p. 148

Wikipedia entry on 'Day of the Dead'

'Day of the Dead', *The People's Guide to Mexico* (<http://www.peoplesguide.com/1pages/chapts/viva/dodead/1dodindex.html/>)

The Guardian, 19 January 2008

Funerals UK (<http://www.funeralsuk.com/>)

61.   p. 149

The Blue Cliff Record, trans. John Tarrant (<http://www.dharmaweb.org/>)

'The U.S. Sub-Prime Crisis in Graphics', BBC website, 21 November 2007 (<http://www.news.bbc.co.uk/1/hi/business/7073131.stm>)

62.   p. 150

George Eliot, prelude to *Middlemarch* (1874)

Encyclopedia Britannica entry on 'Time'

Borges, 'Funes the Memorious'

63.   p. 151

The I Ching, trans. James Legge (1899) (<http://www.sacred-texts.com/ich/>)

64.   p. 152

The Blue Cliff Record, trans. John Tarrant

EVERYDAY SONGS

Texts referenced:

KITCHEN SONGS

Blurb for Gloria Gervitz, *Migrations* (Shearsman Books, 2004)

William Walwyn, *England's Lamentable Slavery* (1645)

Richard Overton and William Walwyn, *A Remonstrance of Many*

Thousand Citizens (1646)

'such is the irresistible nature of truth': Thomas Paine, *The Rights of Man, Part Two* (1792)

Leonard Cohen, 'Hallelujah' (1984)

The Guardian on Barrack Obama, January 2009

Alice Notley on Philip Whalen, blurb for *Overtime: Selected Poems* (Penguin, 1999)

Bob Dylan, 'High Water (for Charley Patton)' (2001)

Peter Riley on David Chaloner, blurb for *Collected Poems* (Salt Publishing, 2005)

Bill Griffiths, *The Book of Spilt Cities* (Etruscan Books, 1999)

DRIVING SONGS

Charles Darwin, *The Origin of Species* (1859)

'When my country …', Thomas Paine, *Common Sense* (1776)

Quote from Palestinian leaders, *The Guardian*, January 2009

Henry David Thoreau, *Walden; or, Life in the Woods* (1854)

Iain Sinclair, blurb for Bill Griffiths, *The Book of Spilt Cities*

Travelodge brochure

READING SONGS

Blurbs and endorsements for the following books:

Donna Stonecipher, *Souvenir de Constantinople* (Instance Press, 2007)

Aaron Tieger, *Anxiety Chant* (Skysill Press, 2009)

Kate Fagan, *The Long Moment* (Salt Publications, 2002)

MTC Cronin, *beautiful, unfinished* (Salt Publications, 2003)

Andrew Duncan, *Savage Survivals Amid Modern Suavity* (Shearsman Books, 2006)

Tupa Snyder, *No Man's Land* (Shearsman Books, 2007)

Sue Hubbard, *Ghost Station* (Salt Publications, 2004)

David Chaloner, *Collected Poems* (Salt Publications, 2005)

John James, *Collected Poems* (Salt Publications, 2002)
Peter Hughes, *Blueroads: Selected Poems* (Salt Publications, 2003)
Charles Tomlinson, *Collected Poems* (Oxford University Press, 1987)

All three sequences written January-March 2009.